Essential American Principles

A User's Guide to American Political Documents

R. Michael Pryor

ISBN-10: 0615766110

ISBN-13: 978-0615766119

Pryolino Press

Printed in the United States of America

To that which I treasure the most, Tiffany

For all of her love, laughter and support

CONTENTS

About the Author:

Mr. Pryor currently teaches in the social sciences, is a freelance writer, and an educational consultant. His goal is to provide the benefits of deeper historical analysis to a larger general population.

Why this book was written

In an age of globalization, the internet, and a 24 hour news cycle; one could argue that the political concepts presented by Patrick Henry or Abraham Lincoln are irrelevant or outdated. Their ideas are simply quaint reminders of America's earlier days, with their messages not as pertinent for contemporary society. However, the ideas and values articulated in these documents are not archaic abstractions; but reflections on how people can create a stable and more just society. The individuals who drafted these documents knew that history did not simply repeat itself; but in reality, what was repeating were the desires and actions of the people.

These political documents are still relevant for reflecting on, and evaluating, the accomplishments (and failures) of a society and their government. The ideas presented in these speeches and writings are just as pertinent today as they were the many decades, or even centuries, ago when they were first created. We, as people today, are very similar to those individuals who lived 150, 250, or even 2000 years ago. American society over the last 150 to 250 years has undergone extraordinary political, social, and economic changes; but the essential question about the nature of government and the relationship to the public is timeless.

This book's over-arching goal is to encourage a basic reflection on the evolving nature of government, while bringing the benefits of deeper historical analysis to a larger general population. The work provides readers with an easy to understand description of key principles from the United States of America's political foundation; principles that are an essential component of the American political identity. Modern citizens must understand how the arguments and concepts from these earlier documents have influenced the American political system and helped to define, as well as change, our very understanding of what is government. This awareness is crucial if people are to critically evaluate and successfully engage in the American political process.

To assist with understanding, the original historical text is presented in italicized "Century" font; with the modern-day interpretation presented in parenthesis with "Arial" font. Each primary source document is introduced by a brief background description so that the reader understands the historical context surrounding each of these political documents.

Prologue

"We hold these truths to be self evident", "Four score and seven years ago", "We the people" -- these quotes are now part of the American vernacular, and like baseball and apple pie; these expressions are now embedded in the American culture. From Patrick Henry's speech to Abraham Lincoln's Emancipation Proclamation, these principles and documents have defined American political history. The very notion of what it means to be an American is, at least partially, shaped by these political beliefs.

A noun is defined as a person, place, thing, or idea. Out of all of these descriptions, an idea is the most resilient.
People, places, and things can disappear or crumble in a few generations, but some ideas can survive for many decades or even centuries. The political concepts and values that exist in these documents have persisted for centuries. The original origins of many of these political ideals and beliefs were from the European Enlightenment during the 17th and 18th centuries. In turn, the principles of the Enlightenment were inspired by ideals from the Renaissance and the Scientific Revolution. The total sum of these historical eras generated unique, and now cherished, ideas about the sanctity of the individual that persist to this day in American society.

There are many other historical writings that could have been included, but these works were left out for convenience and brevity. This book only mentions a few of the documents and speeches that form the central foundation of American political thought, yet even this small collection of writings readily reflect the fundamental notions that are the center of the American identity.

The principles of liberty, rebellion, and equality are still visible in contemporary American society; even though these same political principles seem to conflict with each other and create a

level of tension among the American people.   Ultimately, the
timeless nature of these beliefs is something that readers of this
book should remember as they contemplate the various ideals
presented in these pages.

Timeline of Key Political Events

1492
Christopher Columbus, with Spanish aid, lands in the Caribbean. This initiated an era of European colonization of both the North and South American continents.

1584 - 1587
Sir Walter Raleigh is granted a charter from the Queen of England for lands in North America. However, the first colony (Roanoke), along the coast in southern Virginia, fails and is abandoned.

1607
Jamestown is established on the coast of Virginia, which was England's first successful permanent colony.

1619
The first African slaves arrive in Jamestown, Virginia. By 1700, African slaves will become the primary source of bonded labor in British North America.

1620
The colony of Plymouth is established by English Separatist in Massachusetts.

1754 - 1763
French and Indian War: A military conflict between the French Empire and the British Empire. France losses the war and is forced to surrender most of its North American territorial holdings to Britain (and Spain).

1775
Patrick Henry delivers his speech, "Give Me Liberty or Give me Death". The speech was delivered during a political meeting in the colony of Virginia and advocates open rebellion against Great Britain.

1775 - 1783
American Revolution: American colonists gain their independence from Great Britain. The United States of America is officially established with the signing of the 1783 Treaty of Paris.

1776
Declaration of Independence: The American colonists officially declare independence from Great Britain. The declaration was announced, in part, during the American

Revolution in order to seek international assistance with the war against the British Empire.

1781 – 1789	Articles of Confederation: Created by the Second Continental Congress, this was America's first written national constitution. However, it creates a number of problems and is later replaced by a second document now known as the U. S. Constitution.
1791	U.S. Constitution: Drafted in 1787 and fully ratified by 1791. This document replaced the former Articles of Confederation and remedied many of the shortcomings of these earlier articles. The Constitution also includes the ten amendments (the Bill of Rights).
1795	11th Amendment is ratified: Lawsuits against individual states.
1804	12th Amendment is ratified: Clarifies election of Executive branch.
1812 - 1815	War of 1812: fought between the United States and the British Empire. The war ends in a stalemate and hostilities are formally ended with signing of the Treaty of Ghent.
1861 - 1865	Civil War: A violent and destructive war between the American states. Ends with the formal surrender of the Confederacy at Appomattox Court House in 1865. Settled the legal issue of slavery in the U.S. Constitution; however questions about the extent of federal power versus state rights still remained.
1863	Emancipation Proclamation: Issued by President Lincoln during the Civil War. The Proclamation freed slaves in Confederate-controlled areas and laid the ground work for the 13th Amendment.
1863	Gettysburg Address: A dedication of the Gettysburg Cemetery by President Lincoln. Delivered during a pivotal point of the

American Civil War, it redefined the purpose of the war.

| 1865 | 13th Amendment is ratified: Abolishes slavery in the United States. |

1865   13th Amendment is ratified: Abolishes slavery in the United States.

1868   14th Amendment is ratified: Expands Civil Rights and the concept of due process under the law.

1870   15th Amendment is ratified: Expansion of voting rights to African-American men.

1913   16th Amendment is ratified: A national income tax is passed.

1913   17th Amendment is ratified: Allows for the direct election of United States Senators

1919   18th Amendment is ratified: Prohibits the manufacture, sale, or transportation of alcohol (Prohibition).

1920   19th Amendment is ratified: Expansion of voting rights to women.

1933   20th Amendment is ratified: "Lame Duck" sessions in the federal government.

1933   21th Amendment is ratified: Repeals the 18th amendment (Prohibition).

1951   22nd Amendment is ratified: Limits the number of Presidential terms.

1961   23rd Amendment is ratified: Expansion of voting rights to the District of Columbia.

1964   24th Amendment is ratified: Abolishes poll taxes during elections.

1967   25th Amendment is ratified: Further explains Presidential disability and succession.

1971   26th Amendment is ratified: Expansion of voting rights to 18 year olds.

1992   27th Amendment is ratified: Congressional pay and compensation.

Essential American Principles

Give Me Liberty or Give Me Death

Patrick Henry, March 23, 1775

In 1773, American colonists destroyed 342 containers of British tea by dumping the product into Boston Harbor. This act of defiance, later know as the Boston Tea Party, was considered an act of rebellion by the British Parliament, who quickly countered with a series of laws know as the coercive or intolerable acts in 1774. These punitive laws placed the colony of Massachusetts under martial law and included British General Thomas Gage arriving in Boston with four regiments of British troops.

In response, the First Continental Congress agreed to oppose these aggressive acts by the British government and encouraged the creation of local militias. Pro-rebellion colonist, by 1775, had begun to make defensive preparations for war which prompted the British Parliament to declare Massachusetts to be in a state of rebellion. In hindsight, the Revolutionary War would start by April, 1775 with the battle at Lexington and Concord.

In Virginia, at the time the largest colony in British-controlled North America, a meeting of the colony's governing legislature was held. The governing legislature, known as the Virginia House of Burgesses, was presented the task of deciding whether to mobilize for military action and support Massachusetts, or do nothing and stay loyal to the British government.

A Virginian by the name of Patrick Henry made his famous speech on March 23, 1775 at the Virginia House of Burgesses in Richmond, Virginia. Historically, the speech is credited with helping to pass a resolution that sent Virginian troops to fight against the British monocracy during the Revolutionary War. A political decision that was not only considered an act of war, but also seen by the British Government as an act of treason.

The speech, originally not written down, first appeared in print in 1816. Some of the precise wording of the speech is open to historical debate, with aspects of the speech echoing biblical and Roman history. Famous delegates who were present in the Virginian legislature to hear the speech in person were George Washington and Thomas Jefferson. Both of which would later sign the Declaration of Independence and the U.S. Constitution; as well as become future presidents of the United States of America.

Patrick Henry's "Give Me Liberty..." speech

No man thinks more highly than I do of the patriotism, as well as abilities, of the very worthy gentlemen who have just addressed the House. But different men often see the same subject in different lights; and, therefore, I hope it will not be thought disrespectful to those gentlemen if, entertaining as I do opinions of a character very opposite to theirs, I shall speak forth my sentiments freely and without reserve. This is no time for ceremony.

(Mr. Henry starts out by praising the merits of the individuals who had just addressed the Colonial legislature. He then follows by stating that he disagrees with what these individuals have said and he means no disrespect, but now is the time to be blunt and direct.)

The question before the House is one of awful moment to this country. For my own part, I consider it as nothing less than a question of freedom or slavery; and in proportion to the magnitude of the subject ought to be the freedom of the debate. It is only in this way that we can hope to arrive at truth, and fulfill the great responsibility which we hold to God and our country. Should I keep back my opinions at such a time, through fear of giving offense, I should consider myself as guilty of treason towards my country, and of an act of disloyalty toward the Majesty of Heaven, which I revere above all earthly kings.

(The Colonial legislature needs to, in the most responsible and truthful matter, answer a critical question. Only through debate can we honestly answer this question. If this question, however, is not asked; it would be an insult to both country and God. In the end, I value the King of Heaven more than any nation's king here on earth.)

Mr. President, it is natural to man to indulge in the illusions of hope. We are apt to shut our eyes against a painful truth, and listen to the song of that siren till she transforms us into beasts. Is this the part of wise men, engaged in a great and arduous struggle for liberty? Are we disposed to be of the number of those who, having eyes, see not, and, having ears, hear not, the things which so nearly concern their temporal salvation? For my part, whatever anguish of spirit it may cost, I am willing to know the whole truth; to know the worst, and to provide for it.

(President of the legislature, people tend to hope for the best and refuse to acknowledge the facts. In doing this, people allow themselves to be deceived by lies and slowly loss their humanity. But is this what intelligent individuals do, especially when they are attempting to achieve liberty? People tend not to see or want to hear the action that will save them. Yet, whatever the discomfort, I want to know the truth and prepare for the worst.)

I have but one lamp by which my feet are guided, and that is the lamp of experience. I know of no way of judging of the future but by the past. And judging by the past, I wish to know what there has been in the conduct of the British ministry for the last ten years to justify those hopes with which gentlemen have been pleased to solace themselves and the House. Is it that insidious smile with which our petition has been lately received?

> (We should look at past experiences in order to guide our future actions. In previous years, the past actions of the ruling British authorities, over the last ten years, has comforted members of the Virginian house. But there is a hidden threat behind this seemingly benevolent British authority.)

Trust it not, sir; it will prove a snare to your feet. Suffer not yourselves to be betrayed with a kiss. Ask yourselves how this gracious reception of our petition comports with those warlike preparations which cover our waters and darken our land. Are fleets and armies necessary to a work of love and reconciliation?

> (Do not trust the British peace offers, because this is a deceitful trap. If their intentions were true, then why are they preparing for war?)

Have we shown ourselves so unwilling to be reconciled that force must be called in to win back our love? Let us not deceive ourselves, sir. These are the implements of war and subjugation; the last arguments to which kings resort.

(The British government believes that the only way to achieve peace is through war. Kings always resort to war and conquest.)

I ask gentlemen, sir, what means this martial array, if its purpose be not to force us to submission? Can gentlemen assign any other possible motive for it? Has Great Britain any enemy, in this quarter of the world, to call for all this accumulation of navies and armies? No, sir, she has none. They are meant for us: they can be meant for no other.

(Why else would the British government show such a display of military strength? They have no other enemy in this region that would need this size of an army or navy. This means that the military force is meant to subdue the American colonist.)

They are sent over to bind and rivet upon us those chains which the British ministry has been so long forging. And what have we to oppose to them? Shall we try argument? Sir, we have been trying that for the last ten years. Have we anything new to offer upon the subject? Nothing. We have held the subject up in every light of which it is capable; but it has been all in vain.

(The British government has been slowly taking away the rights of the American colonist. In opposition, the Americans have for over ten years argued for more rights. All of the colonist's arguments however, no matter how well argued; have been ignored.)

Shall we resort to entreaty and humble supplication? What terms shall we find which have not been already exhausted? Let us not, I beseech you, sir, deceive ourselves. Sir, we have done everything that could be done to avert the storm which is now coming on. We have petitioned; we have remonstrated; we have supplicated; we have prostrated ourselves before the throne, and have implored its interposition to arrest the tyrannical hands of the ministry and Parliament.

(For lack of any other solutions should the colonist simply pray? We should not fool ourselves simply because we have tried every other option in order to avoid conflict. We have reasoned, plead, and begged for the British monarchy to protect the colonist from the abuses of the British legislative branch.)

Our petitions have been slighted; our remonstrances have produced additional violence and insult; our supplications have been disregarded; and we have been spurned, with contempt, from the foot of the throne! In vain, after these things, may we indulge the fond hope of peace and reconciliation?

(Our requests and petitions have been rudely ignored and have only resulted in conflict. We have been rejected with contempt from the presence of the British king. We have experienced no success in achieving peace or any level of understanding.)

There is no longer any room for hope. If we wish to be free — if we mean to preserve inviolate those inestimable privileges for which we have been so long contending — if we mean not basely to abandon the noble struggle in which we have been so long engaged, and which we have pledged ourselves never to abandon until the glorious object of our contest shall be obtained — we must fight! I repeat it, sir, we must fight! An appeal to arms and to the God of hosts is all that is left us!

(There is no hope of compromise, if the colonists want to maintain their freedoms for which they have long struggled – they must fight! In the name of God, we must fight!)

They tell us, sir, that we are weak; unable to cope with so formidable an adversary. But when shall we be stronger? Will it be the next week, or the next year? Will it be when we are totally disarmed, and when a British guard shall be stationed in every house? Shall we gather strength by irresolution and inaction? Shall we acquire the means of effectual resistance by lying supinely on our backs and hugging the delusive phantom of hope, until our enemies shall have bound us hand and foot?

(Some people say that the colonies are militarily weak and that they can never defeat the British. But the longer the colonists wait, the weaker they become; while the strength of the British military only increases. The colonies will not gain any military advantages by waiting. The lack of action by the colonial governments is naïve, and will only allow the British to more firmly solidify their hold on the American colonies.)

Sir, we are not weak if we make a proper use of those means which the God of nature hath placed in our power. The millions of people, armed in the holy cause of liberty, and in such a country as that which we possess, are invincible by any force which our enemy can send against us. Besides, sir, we shall not fight our battles alone. There is a just God who presides over the destinies of nations, and who will raise up friends to fight our battles for us.

(The American colonies have been blessed by God. This blessing is displayed by the sheer size of the colonial population. A large, heavily-armed, colonial population would defeat the British. In addition, the colonists have the blessing of God, so they do not fight alone.)

The battle, sir, is not to the strong alone; it is to the vigilant, the active, the brave. Besides, sir, we have no election. If we were base enough to desire it, it is now too late to retire from the contest. There is no retreat but in submission and slavery! Our chains are forged! Their clanking may be heard on the plains of Boston! The war is inevitable — and let it come! I repeat it, sir, let it come.

(The colonies now have no other choice. If they choose not to fight, they will forfeit all of their previous freedoms. This fact is already clear for the citizens of Boston. War against Britain is unavoidable, so we should not hesitate. Again, war is the only option.)

It is in vain, sir, to extenuate the matter. Gentlemen may cry, Peace, Peace — but there is no peace. The war is actually begun! The next gale that sweeps from the north will bring to our ears the clash of resounding arms! Our brethren are already in the field! Why stand we here idle?

(To continue to debate is useless. People may wish for peace, but this impossible because, in reality, we are already at war with England. America colonists in the north are currently fighting the British, why do we not help them? Americans are at war! As Americans, why are we not joining them?)

What is it that gentlemen wish? What would they have? Is life so dear, or peace so sweet, as to be purchased at the price of chains and slavery? Forbid it, Almighty God! I know not what course others may take; but as for me, give me liberty or give me death!

(What do we want as a people? Is the fear of death or the desire of peace worth becoming slaves to the British Empire? May God prevent this from ever happening! I cannot speak for others, but I say let us achieve our freedom or die trying!)

Government is not reason; it is not eloquent; it is force. Like fire, it is a dangerous servant and a fearful master.

-	George Washington

The Declaration of Independence

General Congress, July 4, 1776

The Declaration of Independence formally announced that the American colonies were no longer part of the British Empire. The Declaration opens with Thomas Jefferson attempting to justify legally, and morally, the American Revolution which had already started the previous year in 1775. He states that the colonists have already begun to separate themselves from British authority, and that he must now explain why the American colonists have chosen this course of action.

Many of the Declaration's passages display the influence of the English political philosopher John Locke (1632–1704). In Locke's *Two Treaties of Government*, published in 1690, he argues that if a government does not allow its citizens to enjoy certain rights and freedoms; the people possess the right to replace their government. These concepts, as well as other principles from the Enlightenment, such as the writings of Voltaire (1694–1778), Montesquieu (1689–1755), and Rousseau (1712–1778) are readily evident in this now famous American document.

The Declaration of Independence itself is officially recognized as primarily written by Thomas Jefferson, yet the document was likely a combination of political ideas which were already circulating in the colonies at the start of the American Revolution. During the months preceding July 1776, Thomas Paine's pamphlet *Common Sense*, first published in January 1776, had already gained a large audience by openly advocating independence, as were some individual colonial governments such as Rhode Island and North Carolina.

The Declaration of Independence

In Congress, July 4, 1776. A Declaration by the Representatives of the United States of America, in General Congress assembled.

When in the course of human events, it becomes necessary for one people to dissolve the political bands which have connected them with another, and to assume among the powers of the earth, the separate and equal station to which the laws of nature and of nature's God entitle them, a decent respect to the opinions of mankind requires that they should declare the causes which impel them to the separation.

(There are times in history when people find that they need to change their type government and demonstrate their natural born rights of equality. These political rights provide people the innate ability to separate from their controlling government.)

We hold these truths to be self-evident, that all men are created equal; that they are endowed by their Creator with certain unalienable rights; that among these are life, liberty, and the pursuit of happiness; that, to secure these rights, governments are instituted among men, deriving their just powers from the consent of the governed; that whenever any form of government becomes destructive of these ends, it is the right of the people to alter or to abolish it, and to institute new government, laying its foundation on such principles, and organizing its powers in such form, as to them shall seem most likely to effect their safety and happiness.

(It is common knowledge that all people are equal and that each one of these persons possesses God-given rights. The foundations of these ethical principles are the right to life, liberty, and the pursuit of happiness. In order to guarantee these rights, people must remember that they alone create governments. This means that the authority to rule can only occur with the consent of the general population. This means that the people have the right to change, or destroy, any government that has become abusive. They are then allowed to create a new government based on a set of values that will provide for the creation of a safe but satisfying government.)

Prudence, indeed, will dictate that governments long established should not be changed for light and transient causes; and accordingly all experience hath shown that mankind are more disposed to suffer, while evils are sufferable than to right themselves by abolishing the forms to which they are accustomed. But when a long train of abuses and usurpations, pursuing invariably the same object, evinces a design to reduce them under absolute despotism, it is their right, it is their duty, to throw off such government, and to provide new guards for their future security.

(Good sense should guide citizens not to change long-established governments just because of slight or fickle reasons. People in the past often endured governmental abuse and they did not correct this problem because this was the only kind of government they had known. However, after many years of governmental abuse, where the people have been denied their innate rights; it is the duty of these citizens to get rid of this government and create a newer version that will better protect them as well as ensure their future safety.)

Such has been the patient sufferance of these colonies; and such is now the necessity which constrains them to alter their former systems of government. The history of the present King of Great Britain is a history of repeated injuries and usurpations, all having in direct object the establishment of an absolute tyranny over these states. To prove this, let facts be submitted to a candid world.

(The American colonies have calmly and quietly long suffered from a number of abuses by the British, but now it is time to remedy this problem by changing the government. The British monarchy has repeatedly abused the colonist and behaved like a tyrant. These abuses are proven by the following facts:)

He has refused his assent to laws, the most wholesome and necessary for the public good.

(The King has refused to cancel laws which are damaging to the American colonial society.)

He has forbidden his governors to pass laws of immediate and pressing importance, unless suspended in their operation till his assent should be obtained; and, when so suspended, he has utterly neglected to attend to them.

(Colonial governors are not allowed to make or pass laws that would benefit their local populations. The governor's ruling authority has been revoked until the King can review their actions, but he has failed to review them.)

He has refused to pass other laws for the accommodation of large districts of people, unless those people would relinquish the right of representation in the legislature, a right inestimable to them, and formidable to tyrants only.

(The King refuses to pass any laws that allow for self representation; instead he only creates laws that protect the power of the monocracy.)

He has called together legislative bodies at places unusual uncomfortable, and distant from the depository of their public records, for the sole purpose of fatiguing them into compliance with his measures.

(The King has forced Colonial congresses to purposely meet in difficult and painful environments, with the goal of discouraging any pro-democratic decisions. This harassment prevents the release of any information about these meetings and is simply intended to exhaust and punish the colonial legislatures.)

He has dissolved representative houses repeatedly, for opposing, with manly firmness, his invasions on the rights of the people.

(The King has, numerous times, forced brave colonial legislatures to break up if they ever dare question his abusive behavior.)

He has refused for a long time, after such dissolutions, to cause others to be elected; whereby the legislative powers, incapable of annihilation, have returned to the people at large for their exercise; the state remaining, in the mean time, exposed to all the dangers of invasions from without and convulsions within.

(This continued disbanding of the colonial legislatures has prevented new elections, which means legislative power has now returned to the general population. No matter how many colonial councils and legislatures the

King dismantles, the power of legislative government is cannot be destroyed. The general colonial population now possesses this governing power, however the King's actions has left the colonies leaderless. This lack of leadership places the colonies in danger of both military invasion and domestic disorder.)

He has endeavored to prevent the population of these states; for that purpose obstructing the laws for naturalization of foreigners; refusing to pass others to encourage their migration hither, and raising the conditions of new appropriations of lands.

(In order to limit the population of the American colonies, the King has blocked naturalization and immigration laws; as well as prevented the colonies of acquiring new land.)

He has obstructed the administration of justice, by refusing his assent to laws for establishing judiciary powers.

He has made judges dependent on his will alone, for the tenure of their offices, and the amount and payment of their salaries.

(He has blocked the rulings of colonial courts and threatening American judges with the loss of salary and their occupation.)

He has erected a multitude of new offices, and sent hither swarms of officers to harass our people and eat out their substance.

(He has created new government positions for officials who are pro-British monarchy. These same officials now harass and exploit the American colonists.)

He has kept among us, in times of peace, standing armies, without the consent of our legislatures.

He has affected to render the military independent of, and superior to, the civil power.

He has combined with others to subject us to a jurisdiction foreign to our Constitution and unacknowledged by our laws, giving his assent to their acts of pretended legislation:

(Without colonial permission, during times of peace, he has stationed the British Army in our towns and villages. This military is not under the control of any colonial governor or legislature. Furthermore, the colonists are forced to obey laws that are unfamiliar and strange to colonial legal traditions.)

For quartering large bodies of armed troops among us;
(The King continues to station large numbers of British troops in American communities.)

For protecting them, by a mock trial, from punishment for any murders which they should commit on the inhabitants of these states;
For cutting off our trade with all parts of the world;
For imposing taxes on us without our consent;
(The British Army is allowed to murder American colonists but is immune from punishment. The King has eliminated the colonist's ability to conduct foreign trade and has created taxes on the colonies without their permission.)

For depriving us, in many cases, of the benefits of trial by jury;

For transporting us beyond seas, to be tried for pretended offenses;

(Increasingly, American colonists are no longer provided a courtroom trial with a jury of their peers. American colonists are forced to stand trial on foreign soil for fake crimes.)

For abolishing the free system of English laws in a neighboring province, establishing therein an arbitrary government, and enlarging its boundaries, so as to render it at once an example and fit instrument for introducing the same absolute rule into these colonies;

(In 1774, the British government passed the Intolerable Acts which limited the power of elected assemblies in the American colonies. These acts placed the colony of Massachusetts under martial law as well as limited western expansion into the Ohio River Valley.)

For taking away our charters, abolishing our most valuable laws, and altering fundamentally the forms of our governments;

(The British King has destroyed colonial America's basic form of government by cancelling colonial charters, as well as numerous other democratic traditions.)

For suspending our own legislatures, and declaring themselves invested with power to legislate for us in all cases whatsoever.

He has abdicated government here, by declaring us out of his protection and waging war against us.

He has plundered our seas, ravaged our coasts, burned our towns, and destroyed the lives of our people.

(By ignoring American colonial governments and declaring that the British government is the only ruling authority, the

King is no longer protecting the American colonies and is in fact at war against the colonists. He has stolen from American merchants, attacked coastal towns, and destroyed the lives of many colonists.)

He is at this time transporting large armies of foreign mercenaries to complete the works of death, desolation, and tyranny already begun with circumstances of cruelty and perfidy scarcely paralleled in the most barbarous ages, and totally unworthy the head of a civilized nation.

(The British king is using non-British mercenaries to murder American colonists. This action violates the best of British traditions and is unfitting behavior for an advanced, modern nation.)

He has constrained our fellow-citizens, taken captive on the high seas, to bear arms against their country, to become the executioners of their friends and brethren, or to fall themselves by their hands.

(The King has kidnapped American colonist from ocean going vessels and forced them to join the British navy, where they are then are forced to attack their fellow Americans.)

He has excited domestic insurrection among us, and has endeavored to bring on the inhabitants of our frontiers the merciless Indian savages, whose known rule of warfare is an undistinguished destruction of all ages, sexes, and conditions.

(The King has encouraged rebellion among the colonist and has supported Native American tribes who have brutally attacked American colonists along the western border.)

In every stage of these oppressions we have petitioned for redress in the most humble terms; our repeated petitions have been answered only by repeated injury. A prince, whose character is thus marked by every act which may define a tyrant, is unfit to be the ruler of a free people.

(Americans have repeatedly requested that the monarchy stop these actions, but their request have only encouraged additional attacks from the King. A leader who acts like a tyrant should not rule over a sovereign nation based on the principles of liberty.)

Nor have we been wanting in our attentions to our British brethren. We have warned them, from time to time, of attempts by their legislature to extend an unwarrantable jurisdiction over us. We have reminded them of the circumstances of our emigration and settlement here. We have appealed to their native justice and magnanimity; and we have conjured them, by the ties of our common kindred, to disavow these usurpations which would inevitably interrupt our connections and correspondence. They too, have been deaf to the voice of justice and of consanguinity. We must, therefore, acquiesce in the necessity which denounces our separation, and hold them as we hold the rest of mankind, enemies in war, in peace friends.

(Over the years, the American colonists have repeatedly warned the British government about its excessive control over the colonies. The colonists, due to their physical distance from the British capital, require more political independence. Due to the fact that many American colonists British possess some British ancestry as well as follow the traditions of English common law, the colonists assumed that the British government would respond to their requests. However, a separation from British rule is now required, because the King has continued to abuse the colonists.)

We, therefore, the representatives of the United States of America, in General Congress assembled, appealing to the Supreme Judge of the world for the rectitude of our intentions, do, in the name and by the authority of the good people of these colonies solemnly publish and declare, That these United Colonies are, and of right ought to be, free and independent states;

> (The Continental Congress of the United States of America, with God knowing our intentions, and with the permission of the people from the American colonies, officially declares that the colonies are now a sovereign and independent nation.)

that they are absolved from all allegiance to the British crown and that all political connection between them and the state of Great Britain is, and ought to be, totally dissolved; and that, as free and independent states, they have full power to levy war, conclude peace, contract alliances, establish commerce, and do all other acts and things which independent states may of right do.

> (The United States of America breaks all political connections, as well as loyalty, to the British Monarchy and government. As a free nation, the United States has the authority to declare war, conduct treaties, create alliances, establish trade relations, as well as all other actions that are required for a free and independent nation to properly function.)

And for the support of this declaration, with a firm reliance on the protection of Divine Providence, we mutually pledge to each other our lives, our fortunes, and our sacred honor.

(Through this declaration, God willingly, we fully pledge ourselves to this newly formed, self-governing nation.)

(Signed by)
John Hancock (President of the Continental Congress)

(Georgia)
Button Gwinnett
Lyman Hall
George Walton

(Rhode Island)
Stephen Hopkins
William Ellery

(Connecticut)
Roger Sherman
Samuel Huntington
William Williams
Oliver Wolcott

(North Carolina)
William Hooper
Joseph Hewes
John Penn

(South Carolina)
Edward Rutledge
Thomas Hayward, Jr.
Thomas Lynch, Jr.
Arthur Middleton

(Maryland)
Samuel Chase
William Paca
Thomas Stone
Charles Carroll of Carrollton

(Virginia)
George Wythe,
Richard Henry Lee
Thomas Jefferson
Benjamin Harrison
Thomas Nelson, Jr.
Francis Lightfoot Lee
Carter Braxton

(Pennsylvania)
Robert Morris
Benjamin Rush
Benjamin Franklin
John Morton
George Clymer
James Smith
George Taylor
James Wilson
George Ross

(Delaware)
Caesar Rodney
George Read
Thomas McKean

(New York)
William Floyd
Philip Livingston
Francis Lewis
Lewis Morris

(New Jersey)
Richard Stockton
John Witherspoon
Francis Hopkinson
John Hart
Abraham Clark

(New Hampshire)
Josiah Bartlett
William Whipple
Matthew Thornton

(Massachusetts)
Samuel Adams
John Adams
Robert Treat Paine
Elbridge Gerry

<u>The Constitution of the United States of America</u>

Created -- September 17, 1787

Ratified -- December 15, 1791

The U.S. Constitution provides a basic guideline or blueprint for the American political system. It created a framework for political debate while simultaneously encouraging governmental stability. Born from the ideas of the Enlightenment, it is a document that incorporates ancient and modern political concepts. As a living document, it still continues to inspire compromise, dissent, and admiration among the population of America.

Purpose of the U.S. Constitution:

Parts of the U.S. Constitution	
Preamble	
Article 1	
Article 2	
Article 3	
Article 4	
Article 5	
Article 6	

The original task of officials who met in Philadelphia in the year 1787 was to correct problems with the current federal government. The original goal had been to amend the Articles of Confederation, but they soon found themselves creating a completely new document. A document that would remedy the weaknesses of the existing Articles of Confederation.

In the year 1787, the United States had only been an independent and legally and recognized nation since the signing of the 1783 Treaty of Paris. After separating from an Empire with a monarch, the last thing that most the framers wanted to do

Article 7

Bill of Rights (1 - 10)

Amendments 11 – 27

was create another monarch in the United States. However, the fear of social upheaval and anarchy was a real concern for many of the framers, which inspired them to design the Constitution with five basic goals clearly evident.

Goals of the Constitution:

1.   Establish Legitimacy:

The framers had to establish the legitimacy of the new government which was based upon the newly drafted U. S. Constitution. The framers view of government had been initially presented in the Declaration of Independence in 1776, which had explained why British control of the American colonies was illegitimate. American officials now had to create a legal government that was legitimate according to the standards set forth by the Declaration of Independence. This is why the Constitution starts with the phrase "We the people of the United States . . . do ordain and establish this Constitution." This new political document is a contract between the government and the civilian population.

2.   Create appropriate government structures:

The second reason for establishing the Constitution was to create stable and viable governmental structures. The framers were committed to the basic principles of representative democracy (excluding slaves); however they disagreed over the exact details. Another basic principle was that the new federal government must allow states to possess some local autonomy within their respective political boundaries. In order to achieve this goal, the delegates purposely created a separation of powers for their national government. Power at the national level is divided between the legislative branch (Congress), the executive branch (President), and the Judiciary branch (Courts). A division of power was also created between the national government and the various state governments.

3.   **Describe and Allocate Power:**

The founding fathers specifically wanted to explain and distribute governmental power between the various newly created political structures mentioned in the Constitutions. The powers of Congress are explicitly listed in Article 1, Section 8 of the Constitution, while the majority of the power for the presidency is described in Article 2, Section 2, and 3. Article 3 of the Constitution clarifies the powers of the courts, and article 4 implies that the individual states retain governing authority over public matters.

4.   **Limit Government Powers:**

The authors of the U.S. Constitution specifically wanted to limit the power of the various government structures that they had created. The limits on the legislative branch's authority are described in Article 1, Section 9 of the Constitution. Similar limits on governmental power are located in Article 1, Section 10, which limits the powers of state governments. The framers explicitly stated the function and role of the federal government, with the expressed purpose being that the individual state governments could not take over these functions.

5.   **Allow for Change:**

The framers were familiar with European history and they knew that nations eventually changed. With this in mind, they included a mechanism for adjustment within the Constitution, but this created a dilemma for the founding fathers. They wanted to guarantee that the national and state governments would endure over time, by changing or adapting to the needs to the society; but they did not want to alter the core principles or tenets of the Constitution. If the core principles were altered, the very structure of the government itself could become unstable. With this belief in mind, the framers created Article 5 which created a difficult, but not impossible, method for changing or amending the U.S. Constitution.

Overall, the Constitution is an amazing piece of legislative work yet it is full of compromises. Small states like Rhode Island were fearful that larger and more populous states, such as Virginia, would dominate the national government. In order to remedy this concern, the framers designed the Senate, which gave smaller states the same representational power as the states with a larger population.

Other issues revolved around the divisive, but well-entrenched institution of slavery. Major compromises were included that allowed slaves states to count each slave as three fifths of a person when calculating the number of seats in the House of Representatives. After three years of fiery debate the Constitution was finally ratified in 1791, but only after adding a guarantee of personal liberties known as the Bill of Rights.

How to read the U.S. Constitution:

The original manuscript of the Constitution was printed on a beige parchment paper, is a total of six pages; and is currently located in the National Archives in Washington D.C. For the reader's benefit, each article has been divided into sections, with sections subdivided into individual clauses. Explanatory notes have been added next to each article, section, or clause; with these notes placed in parentheses, while the original Constitution is presented in italicized print. For easier reading the headings and explanations were added while spelling and punctuation was modernized. The portions of the Constitution that have been altered by the addition of new amendments have been crossed out.

Overall the Constitution is divided in to a Preamble, 7 Articles, as well as 27 Amendments. In modern concepts, the "Preamble" is like an introduction while the "Articles" are basically chapters. The 27 individual "Amendments" are just as their name implies, these amendments are add-ons to the original Constitution; with the first 10 amendments known as the Bill of Rights.

When referring to specific portions of the U.S. Constitution, the information is presented in regards to where it is located in the document. This means that every reference will use the words *Article*, the *Section*, and then the *Clause*. So, an *Article* is comprised of many *Clauses*, while a *Clause* may encompass many *Articles*.

For example:

(Officers and Impeachments) *The House of Representatives shall choose their Speaker and other officers, and shall have the sole power of impeachment.*

The example above is located in the first portion of the U.S. Constitution which is Article 1, which happens to contain a total of 10 *Sections*. These Sections of the Constitution are made up of individual *Clauses*, with some Sections having as little as 2 clauses while others possess a total of 18 Clauses. The example listed above is located in Article 1, Section 2, Clause 5 of the Constitution

Constitutional Requirements for Holding Federal Office

Position	Minimum Age	Residency	Citizenship	Location in Constitution
Representative	25	State in which elected	7 years	Article 1, Section 2.2
Senator	30	State in which elected	9 years	Article 1, Section 3.3
President	35	14 years in the U. S.	Natural/native born	Article 2, Section 1.5
Supreme Court Justice	None	None	None	Article 3 (Judiciary)

U.S. Constitution – Contents in Detail

Preamble

Article 1 - The Legislative Branch
Section 1 - The Legislature
Section 2 - The House
Section 3 - The Senate
Section 4 - Elections, Meetings
Section 5 - Membership, Rules,
      Journals, Adjournment
Section 6 - Compensation
Section 7 - Revenue Bills, Legislative Process,
      Presidential Veto
Section 8 - Powers of Congress
Section 9 - Limits on Congress
Section 10 - Powers Prohibited of States

Article 2 - The Executive Branch
Section 1 - The President
Section 2 - Civilian Power over Military, Cabinet,
      Pardon Power, Appointments
Section 3 - State of the Union, Convening
      Congress
Section 4 - Disqualification
Article 3 - The Judicial Branch
Section 1 - Judicial Powers
Section 2 - Trial by Jury, Original Jurisdiction,
      Jury Trials
Section 3 – Treason

Article 3 - The Judicial Branch
Section 1 - Judicial Powers
Section 2 - Trial by Jury, Original Jurisdiction,
      Jury Trials
Section 3 – Treason

Article 4 - The States
Section 1 - Each State to Honor All Others
Section 2 - State Citizens, Extradition
Section 3 - New States
Section 4 - Republican Government

Article 5 – Amendment

Article 6 - Debts, Supremacy, Oaths

Article 7 – Ratification

Signatories

Amendments

Amendment 1 - Freedom of Religion, Press,
      Expression

Amendment 2 - Right to Bear Arms

Amendment 3 - Quartering of Soldiers

Amendment 4 - Search and Seizure

Amendment 5 - Trial and Punishment,
      Compensation for Takings

Amendment 6 - Right to Speedy Trial,
      Confrontation of Witnesses

Amendment 7 - Trial by Jury in Civil Cases

Amendment 8 - Cruel and Unusual Punishment

Amendment 9 - Construction of Constitution

Amendment 10 - Powers of the States and
      People

Amendment 11 - Judicial Limits

Amendment 12 - Choosing the President, Vice
      President

Amendment 13 - Slavery Abolished

Amendment 14 - Citizenship Rights

Amendment 15 - Race No Barrier to Voting

Amendment 16 - Status of Income Tax Clarified

Amendment 17 - Senators Elected by Popular
      Vote

Amendment 18 - Liquor Abolished

Amendment 19 - Women's Suffrage

Amendment 20 - Presidential, Congressional
      Terms

Amendment 21 - Amendment 18 Repealed

Amendment 22 - Presidential Term Limits

Amendment 23 - Presidential Vote for District of
      Columbia

Amendment 24 - Poll Taxes banned

Amendment 25 - Presidential Disability and
      Succession

Amendment 26 - Voting Age Set to 18 Years

Amendment 27 - Limiting Changes to
      Congressional Pay

Constitution of the United States

(Preamble – Purpose of the Constitution)

We The People of the United States, in order to form a more perfect union, establish justice, ensure domestic tranquility, provide for the common defense, promote the general welfare, and secure the blessings of liberty to ourselves and our posterity, do ordain and establish this Constitution for the United States of America.

(For the newly established United States of America, the first federal government was ruled based on the principles from the Articles of Confederation. These Articles were created by a political agreement between the original 13 states. However, the authors (or framers) of the Constitution wanted to encourage its legitimacy as a rule of law, so the document's political power was derived, specifically, from the American people; and not from the individual states which could have decided to withdraw their support at any time.)

ARTICLE I. (The Legislature)

Section 1. (Congress)

All legislative powers, herein granted, shall be vested in a Congress of the United States, which shall consist of a Senate and House of Representatives.

(The first section of the U.S. Constitution begins with the Congress and not the presidency or the courts on purpose. The authors of the Constitution wanted to stress the central role of the legislative branch, or Congress, in the new federal government. This branch most directly represents the people's desires and the ideals of democracy. The legislative branch is the most responsive to the will of the people.)

Section 2. (The House of Representatives)

(Clause 1 - Elections)   *The House of Representatives shall be composed of Members chosen every second year by all the people of the several States, and the Electors in each State shall have the qualifications requisite for Electors of the most numerous branch of the State Legislature.*

> (The House or Representatives was created to most directly express the desires of the general population. The two year election cycle is intended to keep the representative body from becoming static or unresponsive to the people's concerns. The framers decided that two years was a reasonable amount of time for a member to serve in the House.)

(Clause 2 - Qualifications) *No person shall be a Representative who shall not have attained to the age of twenty-five years, and been seven years a citizen of the United States, and who shall not, when elected, be an inhabitant of that State in which he shall be chosen.*

> (The House of Representatives was designed in order to fully reflect the needs and concerns of the American people. The goal was to have the legislative members express the will of their constituents (the people) as closely as possible. To discourage complacency, the framers established two years as a reasonable term of service for members of the House. The framers added age and citizenship requirements to help guarantee that the system was not abused. The age of 25 years old is fairly young, but this reinforces the goal of making the House a more dynamic legislative body.)

(Clause 3 - Number of Representatives) *Representatives and* ~~direct~~ ~~taxes~~ *shall be apportioned among the several States which may be included within this Union, according to the respective numbers,* ~~which shall be determined by adding to the whole number of free~~ ~~persons, including those bound to service for a term of years, and~~ ~~excluding Indians not taxed, three-fifths of all other persons.~~ *The actual enumeration shall be made within three years after the first meeting of the Congress of the United States, and within every subsequent term of ten years, in such manner as they shall by law direct. The number of Representatives shall not exceed one for every thirty thousand, but each State shall have at least one Representative;* ~~and until such enumeration shall be made, the State~~ ~~of New-Hampshire shall be entitled to choose three, Massachusetts~~ ~~eight, Rhode-Island and Providence Plantation one, Connecticut five,~~ ~~New-York six, New-Jersey four, Pennsylvania eight, Delaware one,~~ ~~Maryland six, Virginia ten, North-Carolina five, South-Carolina five,~~ ~~and Georgia three.~~

(In what is known as redistricting, the framers included a mechanism in the Constitution that would allow the government to grow and adapt as the country grew. Originally, slaves were counted as three-fifths of person in regards to a state's allocation of representatives, while Native Americans were fully excluded. The outlawing of slavery by the 13th Amendment in 1865 made part of this section obsolete.)

(This is why the Constitution requires a national census every ten years. The census is the government's way of responding to population changes in the various parts of the nation. In order to minimize federal government interference, each state is allowed to create its own standards in redrawing, or redistricting, congressional and legislative districts. However, recent Supreme Court decisions have allowed the federal government to intervene where fundamental civil liberties are violated.)

(Clause 4 - Vacancies) *When vacancies happen in the Representation from any State, the Executive authority thereof shall issue writs of election to fill such vacancies.*

> (If a representative dies or resign during his or her term in the House, the individual states possess the power to fill this vacancy. However, the new house member would still have to meet the legal requirements mentioned in Article 1, Section 2, Clause 2 of the U.S. Constitution in order to hold office.)

(Clause 5 - Officers and Impeachments) *The House of Representatives shall choose their Speaker and other officers, and shall have the sole power of impeachment.*

> (The Speaker of the House is chosen by the House of Representatives. The power to impeachment shall also reside in these positions.)

Section 3. (The Senate)

(Clause 1 - Numbers) *The Senate of the United States shall be composed of two Senators from each State, ~~chosen by the Legislature~~ thereof, for six years; and each Senator shall have one vote.*

> (After studying the weaknesses of parliaments and senates in European history, the framers of the Constitution feared the possibility of political instability developing in the new government. Particularly after designing a house of representatives that requires elections, and potentially new members, ever two years. To remedy this fear, the framers decided that senators should have a six-year elected term and be elected by the state legislatures rather than directly by the American people.)

(The Seventeenth Amendment, however, in 1913 would change this section of the U. S. Constitution. The American people after 1913 would now directly elect their senators versus the state legislatures.)

(Clause 2 - Elections) *Immediately after they shall be assembled in consequence of the first election, they shall be divided as equally as may be into three classes. The seats of the Senators of the first class shall be vacated at the expiration of the second year, of the second class at the expiration of the fourth year, and of the third class at the expiration of the sixth year; so that one third may be chosen every second year;* and if vacancies happen, by resignation or otherwise, during the recess of the Legislature of any State, the Executive thereof may make temporary appointments until the next meeting of the Legislature, which shall then fill such vacancies.

(The Constitution specifically designed the terms of the senate to promote additional political stability. This was achieved by purposefully staggering the elected terms of a senator. The terms were staggered so that only one-third of the senators are up for elections, and possibly replaced, at any one time. This staggering of elections, combined with a six-year elected term; creates a more stable political institution.)

(Clause 3 - Qualifications) *No person shall be a Senator who shall not have attained to the age of thirty years, and been nine years a citizen of the United States, and who shall not, when elected, be an inhabitant of that State for which he shall be chosen.*

(As was the case with the House of Representatives, the framers added an age and citizenship requirement to the Senate qualifications in order to limit abuse in the system. The qualifications for Senate were purposefully made more restrictive in order to ensure a sense of stability in the national government.)

(Clause 4 - Role of Vice President) *The Vice-President of the United States shall be President of the Senate, but shall have no vote, unless they be equally divided.*

(The Vice President is part of the House of Representatives but possesses no voting rights. However, if there is a tie in House of Representatives during a vote, the Vice President will cast the deciding vote.)

(Clause 5 - Officers) *The Senate shall choose their other officers, and also a President pro tempore, in a the absence of the Vice-President, or when he shall exercise the office of President of the United States.*

(Excluding the position that the Vice President holds as President of the Senate, the Senate is allowed to elect their own officers. If the Vice President is unavailable, this position is usually temporarily filled by the longest serving member of the majority party. Other elected officers include a chaplain, secretary of the senate, and sergeant at arms, who are not senators.)

(Clause 6 - Impeachment Trials) *The Senate shall have the sole power to try all impeachments. When sitting for that purpose, they shall by on oath or affirmation. When the President of the United State is tried, the Chief Justice shall preside; and no person shall be convicted without the concurrence of two thirds of the members present.*

(After the House of Representatives initiates a vote to impeach, the Senate shall conduct a trail in order to decide whether to acquit or convict the accused. A two-thirds vote is required in order to remove an elected individual from office. The chief justice of the U.S. Supreme Court supervises the impeachment trial of a president.)

(Clause 7 - Punishment for Impeachment) *Judgment, in cases of impeachment, shall not extend further than to removal from office, and disqualification to hold and enjoy any office of honor, trust or profit, under the United States; but the party convicted shall nevertheless be liable and subject to indictment, trial, judgment and punishment, according to law.*

(If the person is found guilty, they may be barred from holding future elected positions. They are also open to trial and possible conviction in criminal court. To summarize the overall impeachment process: the entire preceding takes place in Congress; the House votes whether to officially accuse the nation's chief executive of one or more wrong-doings; and the Senate possesses the responsibility of conducting a trial in order to determine guilt or innocence.)

Section 4. (Congressional Elections)

(Clause 1 - Regulations) *The times, places and manner, of holding elections for Senators and Representatives, shall be prescribed in each State by the Legislature thereof; but the Congress may at any time, by law, make or alter such regulations, except as to the place of choosing Senators.*

(Originally, the individual states were allowed to conduct federal elections, but over the years Congress has gradually passed laws that regulate these elections. A dramatic change was the passing of 17th Amendment in 1913. This Amendment allowed for the direct election of the nation's senators, which ultimately made the method of electing of representatives and senators the same. However, representatives are still elected for two year term-of-office cycle, while senatorial terms are based on a six year term-of-office cycle.)

(Clause 2 - Sessions) *The Congress shall assemble at least once in every year,* ~~and such meeting shall be on the first Monday in December, unless they shall by law appoint a different day.~~

(The passing of 20th Amendment, in 1933, permanently altered this section of the Constitution. The amendment specifies the beginning and ending of elected Federal office terms, and stipulated that Congress now meets on the "3d day of January, unless they shall by law appoint a different day.")

Section 5. (Rules and Procedures)

(Clause 1 -Quorum) *Each House shall be the judge of the elections, returns and qualification, of its own members, and a majority of each shall constitute a quorum to do business; but a smaller number may adjourn from day to day, and may be authorized to compel the attendance of absent members, in such manner, and under such penalties, as each House may provide.*

(Members of the House of Representatives and the Senate will determine whether their fellow members are qualified to serve and have been properly elected. In order to conduct Congressional affairs, one-half plus one of each house is necessary to create a majority or quorum.)

(Clause 2 - Rules and Conduct) *Each House may determine the rules of its proceedings, punish its members for disorderly behavior, and, with the concurrence of two thirds, expel a member.*

(The legislative branch, which includes the House of Representatives and the Senate, are each allowed to set their own rules, discipline members, and expel a member.

However, a two-thirds majority vote by members is required in order to be ejected from Congress. The act of censure and other lesser punishments require only a majority vote.)

(The Constitution grants each house of Congress control over its own rules of procedure and membership. As a case in point, the Senate allows for members to conduct an act known as a filibuster. During a filibuster a senator is allowed to stay the floor of the Senate and continue talking for as long as he or she sees fit. This act is performed in order to stop the consideration of a bill he or she dislikes. However, in recent years, a "cloture" rule has been used to end a filibuster, which allows for the ending of the debate if 60 or more members vote to do so.)

(The House of Representatives, by contrast, has enacted rules which limit the length of debates. In the House, a rules committee decides how long a bill can be discussed on floor of the chamber as well as whether any amendments can be added to the bill. Recently, however, the power of the rules committee has been limited.)

(Clause 3 - Congressional Records) *Each House shall keep a journal of its proceedings, and from time to time publish the same, excepting such parts as may in their judgment require secrecy; and the yeas and nays of the members of either House on any question shall, at the desire of one fifth of those present, be entered on the journal.*

(The House of Representatives and the Senate each must publish journals which list bills passed, amendments offered, motions made, and what votes were cast. These journals also contain an accurate account of Congressional debates which are called the Congressional Record. In addition, video recordings of Congressional floor proceedings are created, transferred, and stored in the National Archives.)

(Clause 4 - Adjournment) *Neither House, during the session of Congress, shall, without the consent of the other, adjourn for more than three days, nor to any other place than that in which the two Houses shall be sitting.*

(This clause was added to the Constitution in order to prevent either the House or the Senate from blocking legislation by simply refusing to meet. To avoid one chamber from having to ask another chamber for permission to adjourn, Congress conducts a "pro forma" or a matter of form session in order to meet the three-day constitutional requirement. During these sessions, no business is conducted and they tend to last less than one minute.)

Section 6. (Payment and Privileges)

(Clause 1 - Salary) *The Senators and Representatives shall receive a compensation for their services, to be ascertained by law, and paid out of the treasury of the United States. They shall in all cases, except treason, felony and breach of peace, be privileged from arrest during their attendance at the session of their respective Houses, and in going to and returning from the same; and for any speech or debate in either House, they shall not be questioned in any other place.*

(The members of Congress shall receive a salary for their services. Unless they commit treason or a felony, they are protected from arrest while they are in session. Members of Congress and protected from criminal or civil liability while they are performing their legislative duties.)

(This protection of "Congressional debate" clause is another example of the framers of the Constitution purposely dividing government power between the three branches. A similar principle exists in British parliament which prevents the executive branch of government from oppressing members of the legislature.)

(Clause 2 - Restrictions) *No Senator or Representative shall, during the time for which he was elected, be appointed to any civil office under the authority of the United States, which shall have been created, or the emoluments whereof shall have been increased, during such time; and no person holding any officer under the United States shall be a member of either House, during his continuance in office.*

(No member of the Senate or House of Representatives can be appointed to a judicial or executive office position while serving as a member of Congress. Also, members of Congress may not accept a salary that had been increased during the term to which they were elected. The founders created this clause in order to maintain a separation of powers between the Executive, Judicial, and Legislative branch.)

Section 7. (From a Bill to a Law)
(Clause 1 - Tax Bills) *All bills for raising revenue shall originate in the House of Representatives; but the Senate may propose or concur with amendments, as on other bills.*

(The House of the Representatives has the authority of initiate all tax bills, but the Senate possesses the ability to amend the bill. Both houses need to support a bill for it to become a law. Since the House of Representatives was directly elected by the people and has only a two year election cycle; this branch of government was created to directly reflect the will of the people. The tradition of limiting the power to tax dates back to the English Bill of Rights in 1689, which gave the English Parliament the ability to limit the ability of the monarchy to raise taxes. Eighty years later, when American colonist protested the various British tax acts of the 1760s and 1770s; they were following a well-established British tradition.)

(Clause 2 - Lawmaking Process) *Every bill which shall have passed the House of Representatives and the Senates shall, before it become a law, be presented to the President of the United States; if he approve; he shall sign it; but if not, he shall return it, with his objections, to that House in which it shall have originated, who shall enter the objections at large on their journal, and proceed to reconsider it. If after such reconsideration two thirds of that House shall agree to pass the bill, it shall be sent, together with the objections, to the other House, by which it shall likewise be reconsidered, and if approved by two thirds of that House, it shall become a law. But in all such cases the votes of both Houses shall be determined by yeas and nays, and the names of the persons voting for and against the bill shall be entered on the journal of each House respectively. If any bill shall not be returned by the President within ten days (Sundays excepted) after it shall have been presented to him, the same shall be a law in like manner as if he had signed it, unless the Congress by their adjournment prevent its return, in which case it shall not be a law.*

(Often know as the "Presentment Clause", this clause provides a precise description of how a bill becomes a law. The bill must first pass in both the House of Representatives and the Senate. After this it can either be signed by the President or rejected. If it is signed by the President, the bill officially becomes a law; however a rejection of the bill means that it has been "vetoed". In the case of a veto, the bill is sent back to the Legislative branch where Congress can once again vote on the vetoed bill. If both the House and Senate again vote on the bill and it passes with over a two-thirds majority, the bill overrides the President's veto and becomes a law.)

(The President has ten days, excluding Sundays, to decide on a bill that has been presented by Congress. If the President fails to take action on the bill such as signing it, or rejecting it, the bill automatically becomes a law. However, if Congress is not in session when the ten days expire, the President can "pocket veto" a bill which means that the bill is ignored, and it does not become a law. Congress cannot re-vote on pocket veto bills. The unsigned bill is defeated.)

(Clause 3 - Role of the President) *Every order, resolution or vote, to which the concurrence of the Senate and House of Representatives may be necessary (except on a question of adjournment) shall be presented to the President of the United States; and before the same shall take effect, shall be approved by him, or being disapproved by him, shall be re-passed by two thirds of the Senate and House of Representatives, according to the rules and limitations prescribed in the case of a bill.*

(Congress cannot ignore the legal procedures put in place by the previous clause by simply renaming a bill and calling it something else. Any vote that creates an item that is enforceable by federal law must follow the established procedures which allow for a bill to become a law. The rules from the previous two clauses allow the Executive branch is to check the governmental power of the Legislative branch.)

Section 8. (Powers granted to Congress)

(Clause 1 - Taxation)   *The Congress shall have power to lay and collect taxes, duties, imposts and excises, to pay the debts and provide for the common defense and general welfare of the United States; but all duties; imposts and excises, shall be uniform throughout the United States;*

> (Section 8 list and explains the governing powers that the federal government delegates to Congress, often known as the "enumerated" powers. The first clause provides for the power to tax, protect the nation, and provide for the general welfare of the country. In later years, the 16th Amendment was added to the U.S. Constitution which allows Congress to issue an income tax on U.S. citizens.)

(Clause 2 - Credit)   *To borrow money on the credit of the United States;*

> (Congress has the ability to borrow money by issuing bonds, which creates a debt that the United States promises to pay back at a later time. The Federal government cannot renounce or "write off" the national debt.)

(Clause 3 - Commerce)   *To regulate commerce with foreign nations, and among the several States, and with the Indian tribes;*

> (Clause 3, in Section 8, of the Constitution is known as the "Commerce Clause" and grants tremendous power to the U.S. Congress. The concept of "commerce" includes all people, and nearly everything that they create; as well as the movement of items across the national border, state lines, or within the individual Native American societies. Every form of transportation and communication is covered by this clause. Numerous federal laws are based on the powers which are granted from the commerce clause, such as navigating waterways, business regulation, civil rights, etc.)

(Clause 4 - Naturalization and Bankruptcy) *To establish an uniform rule of naturalization, and uniform laws on the subject of bankruptcies, throughout the United States;*

> (Congress creates the requirements for becoming a citizen, but only the federal government can determine who becomes a citizen. Bankruptcy laws apply to individuals as well as corporations.)

(Clause 5 - Money) *To coin money, regulate the value thereof, and of foreign coin, and fix the standard of weights and measures;*

> (Congress is allowed to create a paper and coin currency. This right is often reinforced by the "Necessary and Proper Clause" from Article 1, Section 8 of the Constitution.)

(Clause 6 - Counterfeiting) *To provide for the punishment of counterfeiting the securities and current coin of the United States;*

> (This clause is an expansion of the powers from the "Necessary and Proper Clause" from Article 1, Section 8 of the Constitution. The goal is to maintain a sound and stable United States currency. By 1865 the Secret Service was created in order to suppress the counterfeiting of currency, and the Federal Reserve System was created in order to regulate the supply of money.)

(Clause 7 - Post Office) *To establish post-offices and post-roads;*

> (Congress has the ability to establish and maintain a postal service, as well as punish those who use the U.S. postal service for unlawful or illegal activities.)

(Clause 8 - Patents and Copyrights) *To promote the progress of science and useful arts, by securing for limited times to authors and inventors the exclusive right to their respective writings and discoveries;*

> (In order to encourage technological inventions and overall prosperity, Congress has the ability to promote and protect copyrights and patents.)

(Clause 9 - Federal Courts) *To constitute tribunals inferior to the Supreme Court;*

> (The Supreme Court is clearly established by the Constitution, while Congress is allowed to create lower or "inferior" courts.)

(Clause 10 - International Law) *To define and punish piracies and felonies committed on the high seas and offences against the law of nations;*

> (Congress has the power to protect the nation and its citizens from pirates and robbers.)

(Clause 11 - War) *To declare war, grant letters of marque and reprisal, and make rules concerning captures on land and water;*

> (This clause explains the extent of the government's power to make war. Additional "War Powers" are defined in Article 2, Section 2 of the Constitution. The act of granting "letters of marquee and reprisal" mean that a government can authorize a private person to attack or capture an enemy ship and bring it before an official court of law for punishment and/or auction.)

(Clause 12 - Army) *To raise and support armies, but no appropriation of money to that use shall be for a longer term than two years;*

> (Only Congress has the power to declare war, while the President is in charge of conducting the war. However, there have been times when the Executive Branch has used U. S.

military forces without receiving a congressional declaration war. In some of these situations the conflict was declared a "military police action" which avoided a vote by Congress. The extent of a President's power to use military force is still an issue of debate in the United States. All funding for the armed forces is granted by Congress which is another "check" on the government's military power.)

(Clause 13 - Navy) *To provide and maintain a navy;*

(Congress has the power to create and maintain a navy. By extension, congressional authority also oversees all branches of the military which includes army, navy, air force, marines, and the coast guard.)

(Clause 14 - Regulation of Armed Forces) *To make rules for the government and regulation of the land and naval forces;*

(Congressional control of the U.S. military is an important "check" on the power of the military and the "Commander in Chief" which is the President.)

(Clause 15 - Militia) *To provide for calling forth the militia to execute the laws of the Union, suppress insurrections, and repel invasions;*

(Congress has the right to create a militia in order to maintain the nation. In modern times, this legal provision includes the creation and control of the National Guard.)

(Clause 16 - Regulations for the Militia) *To provide for organizing, arming and disciplining the militia, and for governing such part of them as may be employed in the service of the United States, reserving to the States respectively the appointment of the officers, and the authority of training the militia according to the discipline prescribed by Congress;*

(Shay's Rebellion in 1786 and the Whiskey Rebellion in 1794 convinced the federal government that an armed militia was a necessary requirement for a strong and stable nation. By 1795, Congress gave the President Washington the authority to use the militia to suppress insurrections. Since the 1790s, presidents would utilize this authority to maintain the political sovereignty of nation during the Civil War and the period of reconstruction that followed (1860s & 1870s), or enforce federal laws during the Civil Rights era (1950s & 1960s). In the 21st century, the role of the National Guard has evolved to include mobilization in both Afghanistan and Iraq.)

(Clause 17 - District of Columbia) *To exercise exclusive legislation, in all cases whatsoever, over such district (not exceeding ten miles square) as may, by cession of particular States, and the acceptance of Congress, become the seat of the government of the United States, and to exercise like authority over all places purchased by the consent of the Legislature of the State in which the same shall be, for the erection of forts, magazines, arsenals, dock-yards, and other needful buildings;--and,*

> (Congress possesses the legal authority to govern the District of Columbia. This governing power has now been delegated to locally elected officials, but is still subject to federal oversight. This clause concludes by stating that the federal government also controls all forts, arsenals, and other places obtained from the various states for the national government's purposes.)

(Clause 18 - Elastic Clause) *To make all laws which shall be necessary and proper for carrying into execution the foregoing powers, and all other powers vested by this Constitution in the government of the United States, or in any department or officer thereof.*

> (This "clause" expands the legislative power of Congress and allows this governing body to use this authority in any way that seems reasonable and proper. The "Elastic Clause" also grants Congress the power to enact legislation that assists the Judicial and Executive branches in carrying out their objectives and duties.)

Section 9. (Powers Denied Congress)

(Clause 1 - Slave trade) ~~The migration or importation of such persons as any of the States now existing shall think proper to admit, shall not be prohibited by the Congress prior to the year one thousand eight hundred and eight; but a tax or duty may be imposed on such importation, not exceeding ten dollars for each person.~~

> (This provision of the Constitution is now obsolete, but was originally inserted in order to protect the trading and importation of African slaves. By 1808, the international slave trade was outlawed while the 13th amendment officially ended the institution of slavery in the United States.)

(Clause 2 - Habeas Corpus) *The privilege of the writ of habeas corpus shall not be suspended, unless when in cases of rebellion or invasion the public safety may require it.*

> (From the Latin phrase that was later adopted by English common law, "habeas corpus" literally translates as "you have the body". The purpose of habeas corpus is to protect citizens from unlawful detention by their government and is essential for the protection of civil liberties. The concept often requires the arresting party to justify any imprisonment in a court of law by producing proof of the alleged crime.)

(Throughout American History, the Supreme Court has interpreted this clause to give federal courts the power to review state court discussions as well as enforce constitutional rights. Traditionally, only the U. S. Congress has the power to suspend habeas corpus, but during times of military necessity presidents have also waved this right. The most famous example was President Abraham Lincoln's suspension of this right during the Civil War.)

(Clause 3 - Unjust Punishment) *No bill of attainder, or ex post facto law, shall be passed.*

(Bills of attainder allow a legislative body to declare that individuals or groups are guilty of an act and impose a punishment on the guilty party. The Constitution states that only courts can determine whether an individual has violated the law. This clause also states that *ex post facto*, or after the fact, laws are prohibited. An ex post facto law declares an act illegal after it has already been committed, or increases the punishment for an offense, after it has already been committed. This is another "check" of federal power.)

(Clause 4 - Direct Taxes) *No capitation ~~or other direct tax~~ shall be laid, ~~unless in proportion to the census or enumeration herein before directed to be taken.~~*

(Traditionally, direct taxes were levies base on land or people such as a "poll" or "head" taxes. During the 18th and 19th century, the Supreme Court ruled that direct, or income, taxes were a violation of the Constitution. However, by 1913, the 16th Amendment exempted the act of collecting of income taxes from this constitutional requirement, which nullified this clause of the Constitution.)

(Clause 5 - Export Taxes) *No tax or duty shall be laid on articles exported from any State.*

> (In order to prevent Congress from being bias against any particular states or region, the Constitution declares that the legislative branch is not allowed to place a tax on goods exported from any state. This includes trade items moving between individual states as well as those goods sent to foreign nations.)

(Clause 6 - No Favorites) *No preference shall be given by any regulation of commerce or revenue to the ports of one State over those of another: Nor shall vessels bound to or from one State, be obliged to enter, clear, or pay duties, in another.*

> (Reinforcing concepts from the previous clause, this section of the Constitution declares that Congress is not allowed to favor one state over another when it in regards to trade regulation.)

(Clause 7 - Public Money) *No money shall be drawn from the treasury, but in consequence of appropriations made by law; and a regular statement and account of the receipts and expenditures of all public money shall be published from time to time.*

> (The various departments and agencies of the government are only allowed to spend money that has been appropriated by Congress. This congressional spending is recorded and is regularly made available to the general public.)

(Clause 8 - Titles of Nobility) *No title of nobility shall be granted by the United States: And no person holding any office of profit or trust under them shall, without the consent of the Congress, accept of any present, emolument, office or title, or any kind whatever from any King, Prince, or foreign State.*

(This clause stops aristocratic tendencies and prevents any government official from being granted a title of nobility by the federal government. This is a clear break from the European tradition of kings, queens, dukes, and barons; and reflects the egalitarian ideology of the American Revolution.)

Section 10. (Powers Denied the States)

(Clause 1 - Restrictions) *No State shall enter into any treaty, alliance or confederation; grant letters of marquee and reprisal; coin money; emit bills of credit; make anything but gold and silver coin a tender in payment of debts; pass any bill of attainder, ex post facto law, or law impairing the obligation of contracts, or grant any title of nobility.*

(The next three clauses of the Constitution protect federal power from state incursions. Often referred to as the "Contract Clause," these provisions prohibit states from enacting any laws that retroactively impedes the right to form and regulate legal contracts. The Contract Clause applies only to state legislation, but not court decisions.)

(The origin of this clause was in response to the fear that states would continue a practice of granting "private relief," which was common under the original Articles of Confederation during the 1780s. State legislatures would pass bills that relieved particular persons, usually influential persons, of their obligation to pay their financial debts. In order to prevent this behavior by state governments, the framers of the Constitution placed bankruptcy law under the control of the federal government.)

(Clause 2 - Import and Export Taxes) *No State shall, without the consent of Congress, lay any imposts or duties on imports or exports, except what may be absolutely necessary for executing its inspection laws; and the new produce of all duties and imposts, laid by any State, on imports or exports, shall be for the use of the treasury of the United States; and all such laws shall be subject to the revision and control of the Congress.*

(All international trade in the United States, whether imports or exports, is under the control of the federal government and not the individual state governments. The states are subordinate to the federal government and not allowed to interfere in foreign trade relations.)

(Clause 3 - Peacetime and War Restraints) *No State shall, without the consent of Congress, lay any duty of tonnage, keep troops or ships of war in time of peace, enter into any agreement or compact with another State, or with a foreign power, or engage in war, unless actually invaded, or in such imminent danger as will not admit of delay.*

(States are not allowed to place taxes or duties on shipping, which include any charges for entering, conducting trade, or remaining in a port. The states are allowed to work together in order to solve common problems, such as water management or environmental pollution, but any final agreement that is reached is subject to final congressional approval.)

ARTICLE II. (The Executive)

Section 1. (The Presidency)

(Clause 1 - Terms of Office) *The executive power shall be vested in a President of the United States of America. He shall hold his office during the term of four years, and, together with the Vice-President, chosen for the same term, be elected as follows.*

(Creates and designates the role of the chief executive and defines the term of office which is four years in length. Interestingly, the passage is silent on the issue of reelection. George Washington, the first president, established the tradition of serving two consecutive terms, with only Franklin D. Roosevelt breaking the tradition by serving four consecutive terms. The ratification of the 22nd amendment now limits a president to two consecutive terms.)

(Clause 2 - Electoral College)   *Each State shall appoint, in such manner as the Legislature thereof may direct, a number of Electors, equal to the whole number of Senators and Representatives to which the State may be entitled in the Congress; but no Senator or Representative, or person holding an office of trust or profit under the United States, shall be appointed an Elector.*

(The sometimes controversial "Electoral College" was created as a compromise between two interpretations of democracy. The first version argues for the direct election of the President by the general population, while the second version believes that the members of Congress should elect the president. In this second version, the selecting of these "electors" was left up to states. The electors are now decided by popular vote. Some historians argue that the original authors of the Constitution created the "Electoral College" in order to provide a check on democracy and stabilize the political system.)

(Clause 3 - ~~Method for Electing the President~~)   *~~The Electors shall meet in their respective States, and vote by ballot for two persons, of whom one at least shall not be an inhabitant of the same state with themselves. And they shall make a list of all the persons voted for, and of the number of votes for each; which list they shall sign and certify, and transmit sealed to the seat of the government of the~~*

~~United States, directed to the President of the Senate. The President of the Senate shall, in the presence of the Senate and House of Representatives, open all the certificates, and the votes shall then be counted. The person having the greatest number of votes shall be the President, if such number be a majority of the whole number of Electors appointed; and if there be more than one who have such majority, and have an equal number of votes, then the House of Representatives shall immediately choose by ballot one of them for President; and if no person have a majority, then from the five highest on the list the said House shall in like manner choose a President. But in choosing the President the votes shall be taken by States, the representation from each State having one vote; a quorum for this purpose shall consist of a member or members from two-thirds of the States, and a majority of all the States shall be necessary to a choice. In every case, after the choice of the President, the person having the greatest number of votes of the Electors, shall be the Vice-President. But if there should remain two or more who have equal votes, the Senate shall choose from them by ballot the Vice-President.~~

(This portion of the Constitution was replaced by the 12th amendment in 1804. In the presidential election of 1800, Thomas Jefferson and his running mate Aaron Burr received the same number of votes; with both claiming the office of president. The House of Representatives finally chose Jefferson but a problem was made apparent. The original Constitution possessed no separate designation for presidential and vice presidential candidates. In order to remedy this issue, the 12th amendment was ratified only a few months before the next presidential election in 1804.)

(Clause 4 - Election Day) *The Congress may determine the time of choosing the Electors, and the day on which they shall give their votes; which day shall be the same throughout the United States.*

> (The Legislative Branch is allowed to determine the time and day for elections. Congress has decided that presidential elections are required to occur on Tuesday, following the first Monday in November, every four years. While the electors of the electoral college meet, in order to vote, on the Monday after the second Wednesday in December; with the two houses of Congress convening to count the electoral ballots on the following January 6.)

(Clause 5 - Qualifications) *No person, except a natural born citizen, ~~or a citizen of the United States at the time of the adoption of this Constitution,~~ shall be eligible to the office of President; neither shall any person be eligible to that office, who shall not have attained to the age of thirty-five years, and been fourteen years a resident within the United States.*

> (With the ratification of the Constitution in 1791, the "at the time of the adoption" portion of the document became obsolete. In order to become president, an individual has to be at least 35 years old and a natural born citizen of the United States; as well as reside within the country for 14 years.)

(Clause 6 - Succession) *In case of the removal of the President from office, or of his death, resignation, or inability to discharge the powers and duties of the said office, the same shall devolve on the Vice-President; and the Congress may by law provide for the case of removal, death, resignation, or inability, both of the President and Vice-President, declaring what officer shall then act as President, and such officer shall act accordingly, until the disability be removed, or a President shall be elected.*

(The enacting of the 25th amendment in 1967 clarified confusion around the succession of presidents. Eight presidents have died while serving in office, while Congress has passed three Presidential Succession Acts in 1792, 1886, and 1947 in order to remedy lingering problems. The enacting of the 25th amendment in 1967 clarified lingering confusion around the succession of presidents, clearly explaining presidential disability, vacancy of the office, and methods of succession.)

(Clause 7 - Salary) *The President shall, at stated times, receive for his services a compensation, which shall neither be increased nor diminished during the period for which he shall have been elected, and he shall not receive within that period any other emolument from the United States, or any of them.*

(In order to grant the presidency more autonomy, Congress is not allowed to increase or reduce the president's salary during the elected term of office. Furthermore, the president is not allowed to receive or accept any other pay.)

(Clause 8 - Oath of Office) *Before he enters on the execution of his office, he shall take the following oath or affirmation:*

"I do solemnly swear (or affirm) that I will faithfully execute the office of President of the United States; and will, to the best of my ability, preserve, protect and defend, the Constitution of the United States."

(The Constitution explicitly states the oath that presidents are required to take before accepting the role of chief executive. However, the Legislative Branch has created oaths for other federal officials such as the office of vice president.)

Section 2. (Powers of the President)

(Clause 1 - Military Powers) *The President shall be Commander in Chief of the army and navy of the United States, and of the militia of the several states, when called into the actual service of the United States; he may require the opinion, in writing, of the principal officer in each of the executive departments, upon any subject relating to the duties of their respective offices, and he shall have power to grant reprieves and pardons for offences against the United States, except in cases of impeachment.*

> (The president, as Commander in Chief, is in charge of all military forces. Interestingly, since the date of the ratification of the Constitution, presidential power has increased and now influences national and foreign policy in both war and peacetime. Presidents also have the power to grant pardons, which Congress cannot restrain.)

(Clause 2 - Treaties and Appointments) *He shall have power, by and with the advice and consent of the Senate, to make treaties, provided two thirds of the Senators present concur; and he shall nominate, and by and with the advice and consent of the Senate shall appoint Ambassadors, other public Ministers, and Consuls, Judges of the Supreme Court, and all other offices of the United States, whose appointments are not herein otherwise provided for, and which shall be established by law. But the Congress may by law vest the appointment of such inferior officers as they think proper in the President alone, in the courts of law, or in the heads of departments.*

> (This clause allows the Legislative Branch to have a say in foreign policy decisions by requiring the Senate to vote by a two-thirds majority on all treaties with foreign nations. However, the executive branch may create "executive agreements" with foreign powers without consulting the

Senate.   However, this presidential power to create "agreements" is intended to only involve minor matters, which has created controversy in the past.)

(The president must submit all judicial and major executive branch nominations to the Senate in order to receive advice and consent. There is no provision for the removal of officers from the executive branch, so this power is granted to the discretion of the president.)

(Clause 3 - Vacancies) *The President shall have power to fill up all vacancies that may happen during the recess of the Senate, by granting commissions, which shall expire at the end of their next session.*

(If the Senate is unable to review presidential nominations due to the fact that they are not in session, the Executive Branch is allowed to make recess appointments. The Senate is then allowed to review the nominations when they return to session.)

Section 3. (Presidential Duties)

He shall from time to time give to the Congress information of the state of the Union, and recommend to their consideration such measures as he shall judge necessary and expedient; he may, on extraordinary occasions, convene both Houses, or either of them, and in case of disagreement between them, with respect to the time of adjournment, he may adjourn them to such time as he shall think proper; he shall receive Ambassadors and other public Ministers; he shall take care that the laws be faithfully executed, and shall commission all the officers of the United States.

(The president will deliver to Congress an annual update which is known as "the state of the Union" address. This is an important function of the president's legislative leadership. The Executive Branch can, and has, summoned Congress into extra or special sessions in order to deal with extraordinary situations. Interestingly, the Executive Branch has the power to adjourn or suspend Congress, but this power has never been used by a president.)

(The Constitution provides the president a law enforcement function over the Executive Branch. However, this is a constant source of tension due to the fact that the president must execute the laws that Congress passes. This means that these laws simultaneously limit and expand the legal power of the Executive Branch.)

Section 4. (Impeachment)

The President, Vice-President, and all civil officers of the United States, shall be removed from office, on impeachment for and conviction of treason, bribery, or other high crimes and misdemeanors.

(The power to impeach a president is the Legislative Branch's check on the Executive Branch. Impeachment allows Congress to deter and punish abuse of power by members of the Executive and Judicial branches. The majority of impeached and convicted officials have been Federal judges; however three sitting presidents have experienced, directly or indirectly, the process of impeachment. President Andrew Johnson was impeached but acquitted by a single vote, President Richard Nixon resigned before impeachment proceedings could begin, and President Bill Clinton was impeached by the House but acquitted by the Senate. No presidents have ever been found guilty and removed from office through the impeachment process.)

ARTICLE III. (The Judiciary)

Section 1. (The Federal Courts and Judges)

The judicial power of the United States shall be vested in one Supreme Court, and in such Inferior Courts as the Congress may from time to time ordain and establish. The Judges, both of the supreme and Inferior Courts, shall hold their offices during good behavior; and shall, at stated times, receive for their services a compensation, which shall not be diminished during their continuance in office.

(This portion of the Constitution creates a third branch of government besides the Legislative and Executive, known as the Judicial Branch. This branch of government empowers the courts to decide cases, while also limiting their power to only certain areas of the government. Interestingly, the concept of judicial review, which is the right to declare state or federal laws unconstitutional, is not mentioned in the Constitution. The principle of judicial review was not established until the Supreme Court case of Marbury v. Madison in 1803. In order to encourage independence, the Supreme Court justices are granted lifetime tenures with guaranteed salaries that cannot be reduced, and are can only be removed by impeachment.)

Section 2. (The Authority of the Courts)

(Clause 1 - General Authority) *The judicial power shall extend to all cases in law and equity, arising under this Constitution, the laws of the United States, and treaties made, or which shall be made, under their authority; to all cases affecting Ambassadors, other public Ministers, and Consuls; to all cases of admiralty and maritime jurisdiction; to controversies to which the United States shall be a party; to controversies between two or more States, between a State and citizen of another State, between citizens of different States, between citizens of the same State claiming lands under grants of different States, ~~and between a State, or the citizens thereof, and foreign States, citizens or subjects.~~*

(This clause has changed over the years with the use of the words "cases" and "controversies" emphasizing the nature of judicial power. The Constitution requires that any disagreement between citizens or states, the involved individuals or parties must have suffered a sufficient injury in order to summon a review by a federal court.)

(Clause 2 - Supreme Court) *In all cases affecting Ambassadors, other public Ministers and consuls, and those in which a State shall be party, the Supreme Court shall have original jurisdiction. In all the other cases before mentioned, the Supreme Court shall have appellate jurisdiction, both as to law and fact, with such exceptions and under such regulations as the Congress shall make.*

(The Supreme Court is allowed to review certain legal cases even though these cases have not been ruled on by lower courts. The Supreme Court also possesses to power of "appellate jurisdiction" which allows the court to review legal decisions made by subordinate state and federal courts.)

(Clause 3 - Trial by Jury) *The trial of all crimes, except in cases of impeachment, shall be by jury; and such trial shall be held in the State where the said crimes shall have been committed; but when not committed within any State, the trial shall be at such place or places as the Congress may by law have directed.*

(Any citizen accused of a criminal act has the right to receive a trial by jury, except in the case of impeachment. The 6th through 9th amendments of the Bill of Rights further explains and expands this right.)

Section 3. (Treason)

(Clause 1 - Definition) *Treason, against the United States, shall consist only in levying war against them, or in adhering to their enemies, giving them aid and comfort. No person shall be convicted of treason, unless on the testimony of two witnesses to the same overt act, or on concession in open court.*

> (This section of the Constitution reduces the ability of Congress to define and use the charge of treason. In this way, treason cannot as easily be used as a way to silence political "enemies." At least two witnesses need to testify in a court of law stating that the person in question committed a treasonable act against the United States.)

(Clause 2 - Punishment) *The Congress shall have power to declare the punishment of treason, but no attainder of treason shall work corruption of blood, or forfeiture, except during the life of the person attainted.*

> (This clause limits Congress' power to set the punishment treason, which is a check on the absolute power of the federal government.)

ARTICLE IV. (Relations between the States)

Section 1. (State Acts and Records)

Full faith and credit shall be given in each State to the public acts, records and judicial proceedings, of every other State. And the Congress may by general laws prescribe the manner in which such acts, records and proceedings, shall be proved, and the effect thereof.

> (Every U. S. state is legally required to recognize the "acts, records, and proceedings" of other states, as well as enforce these rights in each state's courts.)

Section 2. (Citizen's Rights)

(Clause 1 - Citizenship) *The citizens of each State shall be entitled to all privileges and immunities of citizens in the several states.*

> (Each state is required to treat the citizens of other states equally without discrimination. This clause was intended to unite the individual states into a cohesive nation-state, however later amendments and legislative acts would clarify and expand the rights of U. S. citizens.)

(Clause 2 - Extradition) *A person, charged in any State with treason, felony, or other crime, who shall flee from justice, and be found in another State, shall, on demand of the executive authority of the State form which he fled, be delivered up, to be removed to the State having jurisdiction of the crime.*

> (Similar to, as well as, reinforcing the goals of the previous clause, every state's chief executive must obey another state's laws and return any fugitive from justice.)

(Clause 3 - ~~Fugitive Slaves~~) *~~No person, held to service or labor in one State, under the laws thereof, escaping into another, shall, in consequence of any law or regulation therein, be discharged from such service or labor; but shall be delivered up, on claim of the party to whom such service or labor may be due.~~*

> (Originally written to address the topic of runaway slaves, this portion of the Constitution was made obsolete by the 13th Amendment in 1865.)

Section 3. (Adding New States)

(Clause 1 - Admission) *New States may be admitted by the Congress into this Union; but no new State shall be formed to erected within the jurisdiction of any other State; nor any State be formed by the junction of two or more States, or parts of States, without the consent of the Legislatures of the States concerned, as well as of the Congress.*

> (The Legislative Branch is granted the authority to admit newly acquired territories into the Union. These new states possess the same legal status as all of the previously established states.)

(Clause 2 - Congressional Authority) *The Congress shall have power to dispose of and make all needful rules and regulations, respecting the territory or other property belonging to the United States; and nothing in this Constitution shall be so construed, as to prejudice any claims of the United States, or of any particular State.*

> (Congress controls all of the public lands within each state. The majority of this land is located in the western region of the United States. The legislative branch also governs any acquired territories, which currently include Puerto Rico, the Virgin Islands, America Samoa, and Guam.)

Section 4. (Protection of the States)

The United States shall guarantee, to every State in this Union, a republican form of government, and shall protect each of them against invasion; and, on application of the Legislature, or of the Executive, (when the Legislature cannot be convened) against domestic violence.

> (The U. S. Constitution guarantees a "republican form of government" for every U. S. citizen. However, some citizens would not possess full citizenship rights until the 20th century, particularly African-Americans, Native Americans, and women. Congress also grants the president the right to use federal troops in order to protect the states from "invasion" and "domestic violence.")

ARTICLE V. (Adding Amendments to the Constitution)

The Congress, whenever two thirds of both Houses shall deem it necessary, shall propose amendments to this Constitution; or, on the application of the Legislatures of two thirds of the several States, shall call a Convention, for proposing amendments; which, in either case, shall be valid, to all intents and purposes, as part of this Constitution, when ratified by the Legislature of three fourths of the several States, or by conventions in three fourths thereof, as the one or the other mode of ratification may be proposed by the Congress; ~~provided, that no amendment which may be made prior to the year one thousand eight hundred and eight shall in any manner affect the first and fourth clauses, in the ninth section of the first article;~~ *and that no State, without its consent, shall be deprived of its equal suffrage in the Senate.*

(There are two ways to change or amend the Constitution. The standard method, which has been used to adopt all of the amendments to date, is for both houses of Congress to pass by two-thirds vote a proposal; which they then send to the states for ratification.   At the state level, the proposed amendment can either be ratified by the state legislatures or by the special conventions within the state.   An amendment is only ratified when three-fourths of all of the states approve, which is a high threshold to meet.)

(The Constitution also allows for a national convention, when two-thirds of the states petition Congress for such a convention, to propose and debate new amendments.   Again, any proposed amendment to the Constitution can only become law if fully ratified by three-fourths of all of the U.S. states.)

ARTICLE VI. (Supremacy of the National Government)

Section 1. (Legitimate Debts)

All debts contracted, and engagements entered into, before the adoption of this Constitution, shall be as valid against the United States under this Constitution, as under the Confederation.

> (The new federal government assumed the financial obligations of the old government, which had previously during operated under the Articles of Confederation during the 1780s. This was done in order to re-establish and maintain the young nation's financial legitimacy.)

Section 2. (The Dominant Law)

This Constitution, and the laws of the United States which shall be made in pursuance thereof, and all treaties made, or which shall be made, under the authority of the United States, shall be the supreme law of the land; and the Judges in every State, shall be bound thereby; anything in the constitution or laws of any State to the contrary notwithstanding.

> (This section of the Constitution is often known as the Supremacy Clause and establishes a centralized government and national union. The Constitution, as well as all federal laws and treaties, takes priority over any state law. This clause also commands all judges to adhere to this principle when they are presiding over their courts of law.)

Section 3. (Loyalty to the U.S. Constitution)

The Senators and Representatives before mentioned, and the members of the several State Legislatures, and all executive and judicial officers, both of the United States and of the several States, shall be bound by oath or affirmation to support this Constitution; but no religious test shall ever be required as a qualification to any office, or public trust, under the United States.

(All state and federal officials, whether serving in the Legislative, Executive, or Judicial Branches, must take a loyalty oath to uphold and defend the United States Constitution. In addition, no religious test shall ever be required; as well as a declaration of, a repudiation of, any religious belief, shall ever be needed by any public officeholder in the United States.)

ARTICLE VII. (Ratification)

The ratification of the Conventions of Nine States shall be sufficient for the establishment of this constitution, between the States so ratifying the same.

(The Constitutional Convention convened while the government of the Articles of Confederation was still in effect. The Articles of Confederation required a unanimous agreement of all 13 states in order to change any provisions of the Articles. However, the Constitution authorized the new government to go into effect when nine of the 13 states agreed to adhere to the newly-drafted legal framework.)

Done in Convention, by the unanimous consent of the States present, the seventeenth day of September, in the year of our Lord one thousand seven hundred and eighty-seven, and of the Independence of the United States of America the twelfth. In witness whereof, we have hereunto subscribed our names.

(The U.S. Constitution was adopted on September 17, 1787, by the Constitutional Convention in Philadelphia, Pennsylvania. All of the states were present except for Rhode Island, which refused to attend.)

Attest   William Jackson, Secretary

In convention, Monday, September 17, 1787

George Washington, President and Deputy from Virginia.

New-Hampshire: John Langdon and Nicholas Gilman.

Massachusetts: Nathaniel Gorham and Rufus King.

Connecticut: William Samuel Johnson and Roger Sherman.

New-York: Alexander Hamilton.
New-Jersey: William Livingston, David Brearley, William Paterson, and Jonathan Dayton.

Pennsylvania: Benjamin Franklin, Thomas Mifflin, Robert Morris, George Clymer, Thomas Fitzsimons, Jared Ingersoll, James Wilson, and Gouverneur Morris.

Delaware: George Read, Gunning Bedford, Jr., John Dickenson, Richard Bassett, and Jacob Broom.

Maryland: James McHenry, Daniel of St. Tho. Jenifer, and Daniel Carrol.

Virginia: John Blair and James Madison, jr.,

North-Carolina: William Blount, Richard Dobbs Spaight, and Hugh Williamson.

South-Carolina: John Rutledge, Charles Cotesworth Pinckney, Charles Pinckney, and Pierce Butler.

Georgia: William Few and Abraham Baldwin.

If men were angels, no government would be necessary.

- James Madison

The Bill of Rights

The First 10 Amendments to the U.S. Constitution

Drafted -- September 25, 1789
Ratified -- December 15, 1791

Summary: The first ten amendments, which had to be added to the Constitution before the states would agree to ratify the new document, are known collectively as the Bill of Rights. The first eight amendments list personal liberties, which had been specifically requested by the individual states. The last two amendments impose general restrictions on the overall power of the federal government. Here is a brief breakdown:

- 1st Amendment - protects citizens' rights to freedom of religion, speech, the press and political activity.

- 2nd & 3rd Amendments - allows citizens the right to possess firearms as members of a citizen created militia. Also prevents the government from housing troops in private homes during times of peace.

- 4th, 5th, 6th, 7th & 8th Amendments – guarantees the fair treatment of citizens suspected or accused of crimes.

- 9th Amendment - people's rights are not limited to only those specifically mentioned in the Constitution.

- 10th Amendment – states that citizens and states possess all of the rights that the Constitution does not specifically grant to the federal government.

Amendments 1 through 10

I (Religious and Political Freedom) *Congress shall make no law respecting an establishment of religion, or prohibiting the free exercise thereof; or abridging the freedom of speech, or of the press, or the right of the people peaceably to assemble, and to petition the Government for a redress of grievances.*

> (The first amendment protects religious freedom by prohibiting the establishment of an official church or state - sponsored religion. Free speech and press are also protected, although these rights can be limited for reasons of defamation, obscenity, or out of military necessity during times of war. The freedom of assembly and petition are also granted through the first amendment, which includes protest marching, picketing, and distributing pamphlets.)

II (Right to Bear Arms) *A well-regulated militia, being necessary to the security of a free State, the right of the people to keep and bear arms, shall not be infringed.*

> (The second amendment in modern times is often controversial due to its limited wording and the ever-increasing firepower of small arms. Scholars are divided as to whether this provision protects an individual's right to own firearms or whether it deals only with the collective right of the people to arm and maintain a militia.)

III (No Quartering of Troops) *No soldier shall, in time of peace be quartered in any house, without the consent of the owner, nor in time of war, but in a manner to be prescribed by law.*

(This amendment prevents the government from using civilian homes in order to quarter troops, which was a common practice during the eighteenth century. Much like the first and second amendments, this provision limits the power of the federal government; however unlike the previous two amendments, this provision has become virtually obsolete and is seldom discussed or considered a point of controversy.)

IV (Freedom from Unreasonable Search & Seizure) *The right of the people to be secure in their persons, houses, papers, and effects, against unreasonable searches and seizures, shall not be violated, and no Warrants shall issue, but upon probable cause, supported by oath or affirmation, and particularly describing the place to be searched, and the persons or things to be seized.*

(The fourth amendment limits the power of authorities when searching a person, their homes, and similar private places. In to order search these mentioned places the police are required to obtain a warrant from a neutral magistrate/judge. However, there have been times in history when this amendment has been suspended by the federal government in the name of military necessity or the existence of clear and present danger.)

V (Rights of Accused Persons) *No person shall be held to answer for a capital, or otherwise infamous crime, unless on a presentment or indictment of a Grand Jury, except in cases arising in the land or naval forces, or in the Militia, when in actual service in time of War or public danger; nor shall any person be subject for the same offense to be twice put in jeopardy of life or limb; nor shall be compelled in any criminal case to be a witness against himself, nor be deprived of life, liberty, or property, without due process of law; nor shall private property be taken for public use without just compensation.*

(The Fifth Amendment protects the rights of individual citizen from the threat of excessive government convictions. Indictment by a grand jury requires a decision by ordinary citizens in order to place another citizen in danger of conviction. This amendment also includes the concept of double jeopardy which means that when one has been convicted or acquitted, the government cannot place that person on trial again. Double jeopardy includes the principle of self-incrimination which means that the prosecution must establish guilt by independent evidence and not by extorting a confession from the suspect, although voluntary confessions are not allowed.)

(This amendment also includes the legal concept of "due process" which requires the government to observe proper and traditional methods when depriving an individual of an important right. Finally, when the government seizes property to use in the public interest, it must pay the property owner a fair value.)

VI (Right to Speedy & Public Trial) *In all criminal prosecutions, the accused shall enjoy the right to a speedy and public trial, by an impartial jury of the State and district wherein the crime shall have been committed, which district shall have been previously ascertained by law, and to be informed of the nature and cause of the accusation; to be confronted with the witnesses against him; to have compulsory process for obtaining witnesses in his favor, and to have the assistance of counsel for his defense.*

(Any defendant in a criminal cases is entitled to a public trial that must follow relatively soon after initiation of any criminal charges. During the trial, witnesses are required to testify before the defendant, judge, and jury. Defendants are also entitled to compel witnesses on their behalf to appear and testify.)

VII (Right to Trial by Jury) *In suits at common law, where the value in controversy shall exceed twenty dollars, the right of trial by jury shall be preserved, and no fact tried by a jury shall be otherwise re-examined in any court of the United States, than according to the rules of the common law.*

(In an attempt to strengthen civilian rights, the 7th amendment reduces the power of judges by authorizing the right to have a trial by jury during civil cases. The minimum level of "twenty dollars" is so little by current financial standards, that it would burden the federal judiciary to actually hold a jury trial. Instead, various legal devices have been developed in order to permit alternative resolution of disputes.)

VIII (Limits on Fines & Punishments) *Excessive bail shall not be required nor excessive fines imposed, nor cruel and unusual punishments inflicted.*

(The 8th amendment is briefly worded and somewhat vague in the fact that it simply states that government cannot impose a bail or punishment for a crime that is considered unreasonable or severe. Similar to many of the previous amendments, this portion of the Constitution reduces the power of the government and protects the civil liberties of citizens. The "cruel and unusual punishments" clause from this amendment has been the basis for numerous legal challenges from the death penalty to waterboarding.)

IX (Rights of the People) *The enumeration in the Constitution, of certain rights, shall not be construed to deny or disparage others retained by the people.*

(The Constitution does not specifically mention these rights; so they are considered enumerated or unstated rights. These unmentioned rights can be altered by the government, but only if justification for the modification is found elsewhere. For example, the right to travel is not mentioned in the Constitution, but people possess this right. However, this right can be denied to individuals if they are found, through due process, guilty of a crime and incarcerated.)

X (Power of the States) *The powers not delegated to the United States by the Constitution, nor prohibited by it to the States, are reserved to the States respectively, or to the people.*

(The federal government is delegated specific powers in the Constitution, with any other unmentioned powers falling under the authority of the individual states or the American people. This amendment empowers the concept of state's rights, which has possessed a controversial past in American history. Overall though, starting in 20th century, the power of the federal government has expanded considerably.)

Amendments 11 to 27

Added between the years of 1795 to 1992

Brief overview of amendments 11 through 27

11th Amendment: Lawsuits against States (Ratified 1795)

12th Amendment: Election of Executive (Ratified 1804)

13th Amendment: Slavery Abolished (Ratified 1865)

14th Amendment: Civil Rights (Ratified 1868)

15th Amendment: Right to Vote (Ratified 1870)

16th Amendment: Income Tax (Ratified 1913)

17th Amendment: Direct Election of Senators (Ratified 1913)

18th Amendment: Prohibition (Ratified 1919)

19th Amendment: Women Suffrage (Ratified 1920)

20th Amendment: "Lame Duck" Sessions (Ratified 1933)

21th Amendment: Repeal of Prohibition (Ratified 1933)

22th Amendment: Limit of Presidential Terms (Ratified 1951)

23th Amendment: Voting in District of Columbia (Ratified 1961)

24th Amendment: Abolition of Poll Taxes (Ratified 1964)

25th Amendment: Presidential Disability, Succession (Ratified 1967)

26th Amendment: 18-Year-Old Voting Rights (Ratified 1971)

27th Amendment: Congressional Pay (Ratified 1992)

XI (Lawsuits against the States) *The Judicial power of the United States shall not be construed to extend to any suit in law or equity, commenced or prosecuted against one of the United States by Citizens of another State, or by Citizens or Subjects of any Foreign State.*

> (Ratified in 1795, the 11th Amendment was inspired by 1793 case Chisholm v. Georgia. The Supreme Court ruled that a state could be sued in federal court under Article III of the Constitution. However, this amendment was soon adopted in order to overrule the U.S. Supreme Court's decision in this case, and allowed for states to only be sued in state courts. The amendment established the principle of state sovereign immunity, which meant that the individual states were protected from suits initiated by citizens of other states or foreign nations.)

XII (Election of the President) *The Electors shall meet in their respective states and vote by ballot for President and Vice-President, one of whom, at least, shall not be an inhabitant of the same state with themselves; they shall name in their ballots the person voted for as President, and in distinct ballots the person voted for as Vice-President, and they shall make distinct lists of all persons voted for as President, and of all persons voted for as Vice-President, and of the number of votes for each, which lists they shall sign and certify, and transmit sealed to the seat of the government of the United States, directed to the President of the Senate;—The President of the Senate shall, in the presence of the Senate and House of Representatives, open all the certificates and the votes shall then be counted;—The person having the greatest Number of votes for President, shall be the President, if such number be a majority of the whole number of Electors appointed; and if no person have such majority, then from the persons having the highest numbers not exceeding three on the list of those voted for as President, the House of Representatives shall choose immediately, by ballot, the President. But in choosing the President, the votes shall be taken by states, the representation from each state having one vote; a quorum for this purpose shall consist of a member or members from two-thirds of the states, and a majority of all the states shall be necessary to a choice. And if the House of Representatives shall not choose a President whenever the right of choice shall devolve upon them, before the fourth day of March next following, then the Vice-President shall act as President, as in the case of the death or other constitutional disability of the President—The person having the greatest number of votes as Vice-President, shall be the Vice-President, if such number be a majority of the whole number of Electors appointed, and if no person have a majority, then from the two highest numbers on the list, the Senate shall choose the Vice-President; a quorum for the purpose shall consist of two-thirds of the whole number of Senators, and a majority of the whole number shall be necessary to a choice. But no person constitutionally ineligible to the office of President shall be eligible to that of Vice-President of the United States.*

(Ratified in 1804, this amendment was a product of the 1800 presidential election. The election had concluded with a tie between the Democratic-Republican running mates which consisted of Thomas Jefferson and Aaron Burr. The election was eventually decided in the favor of Jefferson, but the uncertainty inspired a change to the original language of the Constitution. The amendment allowed presidential electors, otherwise known as the

Electoral College, to vote for both the president and vice-president candidates on separate ballots. After the disputed election of 1800, the 11th amendment required separate designations for the position of president and vice president, with both individuals required to meet the same qualifications for eligibility as the president.)

XIII (Slavery is Abolished) *Section 1. Neither slavery nor involuntary servitude, except as a punishment for crime whereof the party shall have been duly convicted, shall exist within the United States, or any place subject to their jurisdiction.*

Section 2. Congress shall have power to enforce this article by appropriate legislation.

(Ratified in 1865, this amendment continued the political trend already established by President Lincoln's Emancipation Proclamation, which went into effect during the middle of the Civil War in 1863. The Emancipation Proclamation ended slavery, but only in areas that had seceded from the Union. It did not apply to states that had remained loyal to the United States, or in areas already occupied by the Union army. In order to fully abolish the institution of slavery, Congress proposed this amendment, which also gave the Legislative Branch specific authority to enforce the amendment by the rule of law.)

XIV (Civil Rights) *Section 1. All persons born or naturalized in the United States and subject to the jurisdiction thereof, are citizens of the United States and of the State wherein they reside. No State shall make or enforce any law which shall abridge the privileges or immunities of citizens of the United States; nor shall any State deprive any person of life, liberty, or* property, without due process of law; nor deny to any person within its jurisdiction the equal protection of the laws.

Section 2. Representatives shall be apportioned among the several States according to their respective numbers, counting the whole number of persons in each State, excluding Indians not taxed. But when the right to vote at any election for the choice of electors for President and Vice President of the United States, Representatives in Congress, the Executive and Judicial officers of a State, or the members of the Legislature thereof, is denied to any of the male inhabitants of such State, being twenty-one years of age, and citizens of the United States, or in any way abridged, except for participation in rebellion, or other crime, the basis of representation therein shall be reduced in the proportion which the number of such male citizens shall bear to the whole number of male citizens twenty-one years of age in such State.

Section 3. No person shall be a Senator or Representative in Congress, or elector of President and Vice President, or hold any office, civil or military, under the United States, or under any State, who, having previously taken an oath, as a member of Congress, or as an officer of the United States, or as a member of any State legislature, or as an executive or judicial officer of any State, to support the Constitution of the United States, shall have engaged in insurrection or rebellion against the same, or given aid or comfort to the enemies thereof. But Congress may by a vote of two-thirds of each House, remove such disability.

Section 4. The validity of the public debt of the United States, authorized by law, including debts incurred for payment of *pensions and bounties for services in suppressing insurrection or rebellion, shall not be questioned. But neither the United States nor any State shall assume or pay any debt or obligation incurred in aid of insurrection or rebellion against the United States, or any claim for the loss or emancipation of any slave; but all such debts, obligations and claims shall be held illegal and void.*

Section 5. The Congress shall have power to enforce, by appropriate legislation, the provisions of this article.

(Ratified in 1868, the 14th Amendment, like the 13th amendment; has a direct connection to the Civil War and the era of Reconstruction. In the 1857 Dred Scott decision, the Supreme Court stated that slaves, and indirectly African-Americans, were not legally U. S. citizens. This meant that they, from a legal standpoint, were not protected by the laws of the Constitution. However, the 14th amendment overruled this decision by declaring that every person born or naturalized in the United States was a valid citizen.)

(Interestingly, the amendment's "due process" clause has had tremendous impact on the overall body of U. S. law, since the Supreme Court has used this amendment in order to apply most of the Bill of Rights directly to the states. The amendment establishes that all citizens are entitled to "equal protection of the laws," a provision which the Supreme Court cited in the historic Brown v. Board of Education case in 1954, which ruled that school segregation was unconstitutional.)

XV (Right to Vote for African-Americans) *Section 1. The right of citizens of the United States to vote shall not be denied or abridged by the United States or by any State on account of race, color, or previous condition of servitude.*

Section 2. The Congress shall have power to enforce this article by appropriate legislation.

(Ratified in 1870, the 15th amendment was intended to protect the voting rights of African-Americans and has served as the foundation for legislation such as the Voting Rights Act of 1965. The language of the amendment however, was interpreted in a manner that only granted the right to vote to African-American men. Women were not granted the right to vote until 1920 with the passing of the 19th amendment.)

XVI (Income Tax) *The Congress shall have power to lay and collect taxes on incomes, from whatever source derived, without apportionment among the several States, and without regard to any census or enumeration.*

(Ratified in 1913, the 16th amendment authorized the passing of a federal personal income tax. Interestingly, this amendment reversed the 1895 Pollock v. Farmers' Loan & Trust Company Supreme Court decision which had declared federal income tax laws unconstitutional.)

XVII (Direct Election of Senators) *The Senate of the United States shall be composed of two Senators from each State, elected by the people thereof, for six years; and each Senator shall have one vote. The electors in each State shall have the qualifications requisite for electors of the most numerous branch of the State legislatures.*

When vacancies happen in the representation of any State in the Senate, the executive authority of such State shall issue writs of election to fill such vacancies: Provided, That the legislature of any State may empower the executive thereof to make temporary appointments until the people fill the vacancies by election as the legislature may direct.

This amendment shall not be so construed as to affect the election or term of any Senator chosen before it becomes valid as part of the Constitution.

(Ratified in 1913, the 17th amendment replaced the original Constitutional provision that granted state legislatures the right to select U.S. senators. However, this electoral process had started to experience problems by the 19th century. Disagreements between, and within, the political parties created problems that increasingly delayed the election of state electors which sometimes left states without full Senate representation. Furthermore, Populist and progressive sentiments by the earlier 20th century demanded more direct representation in the election process. The 17th amendment reflected this sentiment by requiring that senators, like the House, be directly elected the general population.)

XVIII (Prohibition) *Section 1. After one year from the ratification of this article the manufacture, sale, or transportation of intoxicating liquors within, the importation thereof into, or the exportation thereof from the United States and all territory subject to the jurisdiction thereof for beverage purposes is hereby prohibited.*

Section 2. The Congress and the several States shall have concurrent power to enforce this article by appropriate legislation.

Section 3. This article shall be inoperative unless it shall have been ratified as an amendment to the Constitution by the legislatures of the several States, as provided in the Constitution, within seven years from the date of the submission hereof to the States by the Congress.

(Ratified in 1919, one of the more well-known amendments, the 18th amendment made the "manufacture, sale, or transportation of intoxicating liquors" in the United States illegal by 1920. Prohibition was the crowning achievement and culmination of earlier anti-alcohol or temperance movements, which had started in the 19th century. Nicknamed the "noble experiment," this amendment failed to achieve its goals, and after roughly 14 years of enforcement, was repealed by the 21st amendment in 1933.)

XIX (Women Suffrage) *The right of citizens of the United States to vote shall not be denied or abridged by the United States or by any State on account of sex.*

Congress shall have power to enforce this article by appropriate legislation.

(Ratified in 1920, the 19th amendment granted women the right to vote. Women suffrage had been a contentious issue during the latter half of the 19th century. By the early 20th century, many states had already granted women the right to vote in both local and state elections. The amendment established a uniform rule for all states to follow in guaranteeing women suffrage for all elections, whether at the local, state, or federal level.)

XX ("Lame Duck" Sessions) *Section 1. The terms of the President and Vice President shall end at noon on the 20th day of January, and the terms of Senators and Representatives at noon on the 3d day of January, of the years in which such terms would have ended if this article had not been ratified; and the terms of their successors shall then begin.*

Section 2. The Congress shall assemble at least once in every year, and such meeting shall begin at noon on the 3d day of January, unless they shall by law appoint a different day.

Section 3. If, at the time fixed for the beginning of the term of the President, the President elect shall have died, the Vice President elect shall become President. If a President shall not have been chosen before the time fixed for the beginning of his term, or if the President elect shall have failed to qualify, then the Vice President elect shall act as President until a President shall have qualified; and the Congress may by law provide for the case wherein neither a President elect nor a Vice President elect shall have qualified, declaring who shall then act as President, or the manner in which one who is to act shall be selected, and such person shall act accordingly until a President or Vice President shall have qualified.

Section 4. The Congress may by law provide for the case of the death of any of the persons from whom the House of Representatives may choose a President whenever the right of choice shall have devolved upon them, and for the case of the death of any of the persons from whom the Senate may choose a Vice President whenever the right of choice shall have devolved upon them.

Section 5. Sections 1 and 2 shall take effect on the 15th day of October following the ratification of this article.

Section 6. This article shall be inoperative unless it shall have been ratified as an amendment to the Constitution by the legislatures of three-fourths of the several States within seven years from the date of its submission.

> (Ratified in 1933, often called the Lame-duck amendment, this amendment modernized the start and end of the term dates for elected federal officials. The 20th amendment to the Constitution reduced the original four month period between the November elections and the March, which is the starting date of both congressional and presidential terms. If a presidential election was forced into the House of Representatives following a deadlock in the January 6 counting of electoral ballots, that decision would be made by a newly elected House, rather than one set to go out of existence on March 4. It also deals with scenarios in which the President-elect dies or is unable to taking office. In this case, the vice president-elect assumes the position of president-elect and is sworn into office on January 20.)

XXI (Repeal of Prohibition) Section 1. The eighteenth article of amendment to the Constitution of the United States is hereby repealed.

Section 2. The transportation or importation into any State, Territory, or possession of the United States for delivery or use *therein of intoxicating liquors, in violation of the laws thereof, is hereby prohibited.*

Section 3.   This article shall be inoperative unless it shall have been ratified as an amendment to the Constitution by conventions in the several States, as provided in the Constitution, within seven years from the date of the submission hereof to the States by the Congress.

(Ratified in 1933, the 21th amendment repealed the 18th amendment which had created Prohibition. Interestingly, this was the only time in U. S. history that an amendment was ratified by special state Constitutional conventions rather than by state legislatures.)

XXII (Limit on Presidential Terms) *Section 1. No person shall be elected to the office of the President more than twice, and no person who has held the office of President, or acted as President, for more than two years of a term to which some other person was elected President shall be elected to the office of the President more than once. But this Article shall not apply to any person holding the office of President, when this Article was proposed by the Congress, and shall not prevent any person who may be holding the office of President, or acting as President, during the term within which this Article becomes operative from holding the office of President or acting as President during the remainder of such term.*

Section 2. This article shall be inoperative unless it shall have been ratified as an amendment to the Constitution by the legislatures of three-fourths of the several States within seven years from the date of its submission to the States by the Congress.

> (Ratified in 1951, the 22nd amendment authorized that a president could serve no more than two terms, a tradition that George Washington had started in the late 18th century. Before the passage of this amendment, the only president to break this tradition was Franklin D. Roosevelt who was serving a fourth consecutive term as president before he died in 1945.)

XXIII (Voting in District of Columbia) *Section 1. The District constituting the seat of Government of the United States shall appoint in such manner as the Congress may direct: A number of electors of President and Vice President equal to the whole number of Senators and Representatives in Congress to which the District would be entitled if it were a State, but in no event more than the least populous State; they shall be in addition to those appointed by the States, but they shall be considered, for the purposes of the election of President and Vice President, to be electors appointed by a State; and they shall meet in the District and perform such duties as provided by the twelfth article of amendment.*

Section 2. The Congress shall have power to enforce this article by appropriate legislation.

> (Ratified in 1961, the 23rd amendment created a federal election district out of the District of Columbia. Washington D.C., as a functional capital of the nation, was not completed until the late 1790s; years after the ratification of the Constitution. This meant that the original language of the Constitution made no allowance for people living in this area to vote. The 23rd amendment

remedied this oversight by granting residents of D.C. their first opportunity to vote in the 1964 presidential election.)

XXIV (Abolition of Poll Taxes) *Section 1. The right of citizens of the United States to vote in any primary or other election for President or Vice President for electors for President or Vice President, or for Senator or Representative in Congress, shall not be denied or abridged by the United States or any State by reason of failure to pay any poll tax or other tax.*

Section 2. The Congress shall have power to enforce this article by appropriate legislation

(Ratified in 1964, the 24th amendment nullified any remaining property or tax qualifications for voting. An extension of the principles from the Civil Rights activism of the late 1950s and early 1960s, this amendment eliminated polling taxes, which had been used for many decades to disenfranchise African-American voters. Congress was also granted the authority to enforce this provision, which later inspired other voting rights legislative acts.)

XXV (Presidential Disability & Succession) Section 1. In case of the removal of the President from office or of his death or resignation, the Vice President shall become President.

(The first president to die in office was William Henry Harrison in 1840, which meant that his vice president John Tyler became the next president. This portion of the amendment simply formalizes what was already historic precedent and standard operating practice.)

Section 2. Whenever there is a vacancy in the office of the Vice President, the President shall nominate a Vice President who shall take office upon confirmation by a majority vote of both Houses of Congress.

(Before this portion of the 25th Amendment was adopted, there was no legal apparatus to replace a Vice President vacancy; even though this position had become vacant many times in the past. Any vacancy is now filled by a nominee, who the president chooses, who is then must be confirmed by Congress.)

Section 3. Whenever the President transmits to the President pro tempore of the Senate and the Speaker of the House of Representatives his written declaration that he is unable to discharge the powers and duties of his office, and until he transmits to them a written declaration to the contrary, such powers and duties shall be discharged by the Vice President as Acting President.

(A written declaration is required from a president in order to discharge him or her of power.)

Section 4. Whenever the Vice President and a majority of either the principal officers of the executive departments or of such other body as Congress may by law provide, transmit to the President pro tempore of the Senate and the Speaker of the House of Representatives their written declaration that the President is unable to discharge the powers and duties of his office, the Vice President shall immediately assume the powers and duties of the office as Acting President.

(This portion of the 25th Amendment formerly allows the Vice President and a majority of either "the principal officers of the executive departments" or of "such other body as Congress may by law provide" to declare a president disabled by submitting a written declaration to the President pro tempore of the Senate and the Speaker of the House of Representatives. This provision is needed in case a president became incapacitated and was unable to release himself from his duties by providing a written declaration.)

Thereafter, when the President transmits to the President pro tempore of the Senate and the Speaker of the House of Representatives his written declaration that no inability exists, he shall resume the powers and duties of his office unless the Vice President and a majority of either the principal officers of the executive department or of such other body as Congress may by law provide, transmit within four days to the President pro tempore of the Senate and the Speaker of the House of Representatives their written declaration that the President is unable to discharge the powers and duties of his office. Thereupon Congress shall decide the issue, assembling within forty-eight hours for that purpose if not in session. If the Congress, within twenty-one days after receipt of the latter written declaration, or, if Congress is not in session, within twenty-one days after Congress is required to assemble, determines by two-thirds vote of both Houses that the President is unable to discharge the powers and duties of his office, the Vice President shall continue to discharge the same as Acting President; otherwise, the President shall resume the powers and duties of his office.

(Ratified in 1967, the 25th amendment was a response to the recent assassination of John F. Kennedy. Overall, the amendment clarifies the Constitution's previously ambiguous language about presidential succession. It explains and elaborates on the long-standing custom that when a president dies in office, the vice president becomes the actual president; instead of acting as a temporary president. If the vice president position becomes vacant, the president may then nominate a new vice president; who is subject to confirmation by both the House of Representatives and the Senate. The 23rd amendment also provides instructions for replacing a president who becomes incapacitated and is no longer able to serve as president.)

XXVI (18-Year-Old Voting Rights) *Section 1. The right of citizens of the United States, who are eighteen years of age or older, to vote shall not be denied or abridged by the United States or by any State on account of age.*

Section 2. The Congress shall have power to enforce this article by appropriate legislation.

(Ratified in 1971, the 26th amendment lowered the state and federal voting age to 18 years old. Largely passed in response to the military draft implemented during the Vietnam War, the age of 18 was the same age at which young men could be drafted into military service.)

XXVII (Congressional Pay) *No law varying the compensation for the services of the Senators and Representatives shall take effect, until an election of Representatives shall have intervened.*

(The 27th amendment was finally ratified and added to the Constitution in 1992, even though it was first proposed over two hundred years ago as part of the original Bill of

Rights. The amendment does not allow members of Congress to receive an increase in salary until after the next legislative elections have been held.)

The past does not repeat itself, but it often rhymes.

-    Mark Twain

Emancipation Proclamation

Enacted -- January 1, 1863

One of the most famous executive orders in American history, the Emancipation Proclamation was issued in the midst of the Civil War by President Abraham Lincoln in 1863. Before the issuing of the Proclamation, Radical Republicans (anti-slavery) in Congress had begun to pass laws which were intended to eventually free all slaves and end the institution of slavery. However, during Lincoln first year as President, he believed that such laws were unconstitutional and actually refused to enforce them. As a shrewd politician, Lincoln did not want to anger any Northern voters who were sympathetic to the Southern cause.

Yet, by the end of 1862, Lincoln's political views started to change; with the wartime president feeling that further action was needed. He used his authority as the commander in chief to authorize the Union army to confiscate, or free, any slaves that the army came across during the military campaigns in the South. The political logic of these Confiscation Acts culminated with the passing of Emancipation Proclamation, with the first portion of the proclamation released on September 22, 1862. This was a preliminary announcement that outlined the intent of the second half of the Emancipation Proclamation, which officially went into effect 100 days later on January 1, 1863.

Interestingly, the proclamation only applied to the Confederate states that were in rebellion against the U. S. in 1863. This means that the legal order did not include slave-owning areas currently under control by the Union forces or any border states that never joined the Confederacy. Ultimately, the Emancipation

Proclamation created the framework for the freeing of almost four million people held in bondage and dedicated the United States government to ending the practice of slavery.

Abraham Lincoln's Emancipation Proclamation:

"Whereas, on the twenty-second day of September, in the year of our Lord one thousand eight hundred and sixty-two, a proclamation was issued by the President of the United States, containing, among other things, the following, to wit:

That on the first day of January, in the year of our Lord one thousand eight hundred and sixty-three, all persons held as slaves within any State or designated part of a State, the people whereof shall then be in rebellion against the United States, shall be then, thenceforward, and forever free; and the Executive Government of the United States, including the military and naval authority thereof, will recognize and maintain the freedom of such persons, and will do no act or acts to repress such persons, or any of them, in any efforts they may make for their actual freedom.

> (As of January 1, 1863, all slaves in states that rebelled against the United States are free. The U. S. government, and its military, will recognize and assist these former slaves and will take no action that could restrict their freedom.)

"That the Executive will, on the first day of January aforesaid, by proclamation, designate the States and parts of States, if any, in which the people thereof, respectively, shall then be in rebellion against the United States; and the fact that any State, or the people thereof, shall on that day be, in good faith, represented in the Congress of the United States by

members chosen thereto at elections wherein a majority of the qualified voters of such State shall have participated, shall, in the absence of strong countervailing testimony, be deemed conclusive evidence that such State, and the people thereof, are not then in rebellion against the United States."

(By presidential decry, on January 1st, this executive order goes into effect in any state or section of the United States that is in rebellion, unless evidence is provided that proves that this area did not rebel. If this is the case, this presidential decry will not go into effect in these areas.)

Now, therefore I, Abraham Lincoln, President of the United States, by virtue of the power in me vested as Commander-in-Chief, of the Army and Navy of the United States in time of actual armed rebellion against the authority and government of the United States, and as a fit and necessary war measure for suppressing said rebellion, do, on this first day of January, in the year of our Lord one thousand eight hundred and sixty-three, and in accordance with my purpose so to do publicly proclaimed for the full period of one hundred days, from the day first above mentioned, order and designate as the States and parts of States wherein the people thereof respectively, are this day in rebellion against the United States, the following, to wit:

(Lincoln, as the commander in chief of the United States military, stated that the Constitution grants the president the power to put down any rebellion against the national government. A legal precedent, that was initially established during the federal government's response to the Whiskey Rebellion in 1794, this presidential wartime order went into full effect on January 1, 1863; before this time, citizens possess a full one hundred days to contemplate this new law. After these one hundred days, all citizens in rebellion against the United States must obey this law.)

Arkansas, Texas, Louisiana, (except the Parishes of St. Bernard, Plaquemines, Jefferson, St. John, St. Charles, St. James Ascension, Assumption, Terrebonne, Lafourche, St. Mary, St. Martin, and Orleans, including the City of New Orleans) Mississippi, Alabama, Florida, Georgia, South Carolina, North Carolina, and Virginia, (except the forty-eight counties designated as West Virginia, and also the counties of Berkley, Accomac, Northampton, Elizabeth City, York, Princess Ann, and Norfolk, including the cities of Norfolk and Portsmouth), and which excepted parts, are for the present, left precisely as if this proclamation were not issued.

(All of the Confederate states, except for the areas controlled by the Union army, are impacted under this proclamation. The excluded areas, where the newly issued proclamation did not apply were all four of the border states, which included Missouri, Kentucky, Maryland, and Delaware; the Louisiana delta region; West Virginia; Tennessee; and the portions of the coastal plains in Eastern Virginia.)

And by virtue of the power, and for the purpose aforesaid, I do order and declare that all persons held as slaves within said designated States, and parts of States, are, and henceforward shall be free; and that the Executive government of the United States, including the military and naval authorities thereof, will recognize and maintain the freedom of said persons.

(By the power of the presidency, all people held as slaves within these designated areas are free. The United States military officially recognizes and will ensure the freedom of these newly freed people.)

And I hereby enjoin upon the people so declared to be free to abstain from all violence, unless in necessary self-defence; and I recommend to them that, in all cases when allowed, they labor faithfully for reasonable wages.

(All newly freed people should not engage in violence unless it is necessary for self defense and should ask to receive wages for their work.)

And I further declare and make known, that such persons of suitable condition, will be received into the armed service of the United States to garrison forts, positions, stations, and other places, and to man vessels of all sorts in said service.

(Former slaves who are in fit enough condition can now join the United States military. Interestingly, the proclamation says nothing about arming former slaves and having them fight.)

And upon this act, sincerely believed to be an act of justice, warranted by the Constitution, upon military necessity, I invoke the considerate judgment of mankind, and the gracious favor of Almighty God.

(Lincoln closes by stating that the proclamation is an act of justice, allowed under the U.S. Constitution, and a military necessity. May our actions receive the kindness judgment from the people and the blessing of God.)

In witness whereof, I have hereunto set my hand and caused the seal of the United States to be affixed.

Done at the City of Washington, this first day of January, in the year of our Lord one thousand eight hundred and sixty three, and of the Independence of the United States of America the eighty-seventh.

By the President: Abraham Lincoln
William H. Seward, Secretary of State.

"America will never be destroyed from the outside. If we falter and loss our freedoms, it will be because we destroyed ourselves."

- Abraham Lincoln

Gettysburg Address

Delivered -- November 19, 1863

Delivered by President Abraham Lincoln at the dedication of a cemetery at Gettysburg, Pennsylvania; this address is one of the most famous speeches in United States history. The speech was intended to commemorate the fallen Union Army soldiers buried there, while reinforcing the basic principles of American democracy. President Lincoln's short speech is still considered one of the most poetic expressions of American ideals ever articulated.

The Battle of Gettysburg had occurred less than five months earlier and had ended with a resounding Northern victory. In this brief speech, Lincoln appeals to the principles of equality mentioned in the Declaration of Independence, while simultaneously redefining the political and social reasons for the Civil War which occurred from 1861 to 1865.

Abraham Lincoln's Gettysburg Address:

Four score and seven years ago our fathers brought forth on this continent a new nation, conceived in liberty and dedicated to the proposition that all men are created equal.

("Four score and seven years ago" refers to the fact that eight-seven years earlier, the United States was initially established with the signing of the Declaration of Independence by the founding "fathers." Success in the Revolutionary War fully legitimatized America's sovereignty as a new nation with the 1783 Treaty of Paris. The iconic phrase "all men are created equal" was first used in the Declaration of Independence and was originally intended as a rejection of a monarchy. However, slavery was a vital aspect of the young American economy in the first half of the 19th century.)

Now we are engaged in a great civil war, testing whether that nation or any nation so conceived and so dedicated can long endure. We are met on a great battlefield of that war. We have come to dedicate a portion of that field as a final resting-place for those who here gave their lives that that nation might live. It is altogether fitting and proper that we should do this. But in a larger sense, we cannot dedicate, we cannot consecrate, we cannot hallow this ground.

(Lincoln directly mentions the struggles and sacrifices that the Civil War was creating for a nation founded on the principle of democracy, and hints that the United States as a nation could fail. He then refers to the Battle of Gettysburg and states that the Union soldiers sacrificed their lives so that the United States would not collapse or disintegrate. Lincoln honors the dead soldiers, but despises the bloodshed of the Civil War and the country's overall current state of affairs.)

The brave men, living and dead who struggled here have consecrated it far above our poor power to add or detract. The world will little note nor long remember what we say here, but it can never forget what they did here. It is for us the living rather to be dedicated here to the unfinished work which they who fought here have thus far so nobly advanced.

("The brave men" refers to the Union army soldiers who participated in the Battle of Gettysburg, whose actions are beyond the judgment of any political speech. Lincoln continues by stating that speeches made after the battle will be forgotten, but the actions of the soldiers will be remembered. The speech he gave, ironically, was remembered while the details of the battle itself are not as well-known by the general American public.)

(The Union Army's victory at Gettysburg in July of 1863, was a pivotal event during the Civil War; a fact that Lincoln knew when he delivered the address in November of that same year. With the defeat and retreat of General Lee's army at Gettysburg, it was clear that the Confederate Army was losing momentum in the war.)

It is rather for us to be here dedicated to the great task remaining before us -- that from these honored dead we take increased devotion to that cause for which they gave the last full measure of devotion--that we here highly resolve that these dead shall not have died in vain, that this nation under God shall have a new birth of freedom, and that government of the people, by the people, for the people shall not perish from the earth.

("The great task remaining before us" references the Civil War which started in April of 1861, and by the time of the Gettysburg address; had been raging across the American countryside for two and half years. Lincoln, again, refers to the soldiers who perished at the Battle of Gettysburg and reinforces the fact that these men's death will serve a higher purpose -- a new beginning or "a new birth of freedom" for the United States. The final line of the speech reassures the American listeners that the representative democracy of the United States will not collapse or "perish from the earth.")

Significance of the Gettysburg Address:

President Lincoln, in just over two minutes, redefined the American Civil War as not only a conflict over federal power versus state's rights, but as a struggle over the nature of equality which was first expressed in the Declaration of Independence. By the end of the speech, Lincoln had made clear that the United States would become a nation of unified states under one dominant federal government; versus a nation of separate states co-existing to form an individual country.

The Gettysburg Address has remained one of the most famous speeches in American history and was later referenced in one of the most famous speeches of the 20th century. In Martin Luther King, Jr.'s famous 1963 "I Have a Dream" speech, which was delivered on the steps of the Lincoln Memorial; King directly mentions Lincoln's Gettysburg Address. "Five score years ago, a great American, in whose symbolic shadow we stand today, signed the Emancipation Proclamation. This momentous decree came as a great beacon light of hope to millions of Negro slaves who had been seared in the flames of withering injustice." The Civil Rights movement of the late 1950s and early 1960s was an extension of the hopes, dreams, and promises first made by both the Emancipation Proclamation and the Gettysburg Address.

Brief Summary of Voting Rights

From 1789 to 1971

1789 – Male property owners:

At the initial legal establishing of the United States of America's government, only land holding males could vote. However, over the decades and the country's borders and population expanded; this property qualification for voting was altered to include all white males who pay taxes.

For the most part, women were not allowed to vote. The individual state constitutions usually required all voters to be a white male and at least 21 years of age. By the 1840s, due to the waving of land ownership as a voting requirement, the vast majority of white males, whether wealthier landowners or poorer landless men; could vote in the United States.

1870 – African – American Males:

The 15th Amendment to the U.S. Constitution provided the right to vote to all African-American males. The amendment stated that the right of citizens "to vote shall not be denied or abridged by the United States or by any state on account of race, color, or previous condition of servitude." This amendment was a continuation of the new rights granted in the 13th (abolishes slavery) and 14th amendments (civil rights). However, years after the passing of this amendment, African-American men were often not allowed to vote due to the use of poll taxes and literacy test. These practices, however, were legally abolished by the 24th Amendment (poll taxes) in 1964 and the Voting Rights Act of 1965 (literacy tests).

1920 – Woman Suffrage:

Women were finally granted the right to vote with the ratification of the 19th Amendment. Before this, the Constitution had allowed individual states to determine voting qualifications for women. The first national women's rights convention in the United Sates was held in Seneca Falls, New York in 1848. A women's voting rights (suffrage) amendment was introduced in 1878, but was not fully adopted, ratified, and added to the Constitution until August 18, 1920.

1924 – Native Americans:

After World War I, the Federal government had sought to fully assimilate Native Americans. Some American Indians had already been granted citizenship through marriage, military service, or special statutes. By 1924, the U. S. Congress finally granted full citizenship and voting rights to all Native Americans born in the United States. However, a few states would not provide full voting rights to Native Americans until 1948.

1971 – Eighteen-year-old vote:

The legal right to vote became a major issue during the 1960s, in large part because of the Vietnam War. Americans started questioning the fact that 18-year-olds were drafted in order to fight in Vietnam, but they were not allowed to vote. In response to students protesting the Vietnam War, as well as recent Supreme Court decisions, the 26th Amendment lowered the minimum voting age in the United States to 18 on July 1, 1971. Before this, the minimum voting age had been 21 years of age.

Bibliography

Published works:

Brinkley, Alan. <u>American History: A Survey</u> 11th ed. (New York: McGraw-Hill Humanities), 2003.

Carnes, Mark C., & Garraty, John A. <u>The American Nation: A History of the United States</u>, Volume 1, 14th ed. (New York: Prentice Hall), 2011.

Divine, Robert A. et al. <u>America: Past and Present</u>, 7th ed. (New York: Pearson Longman), 2004

Faragher, John Mack, et al. <u>Out of Many: A History of the American People</u>, Brief Edition, Combined Volume, 6th ed. (New York: Pearson), 2011

Internet sources:

Cornell University
www.law.cornell.edu/constitution/overview

United States National Archives.
www.archives.gov/historical-docs/

Yale Law School.
http://avalon.law.yale.edu/

Also by R. Michael Pryor

Alexander McGillivray and the Creek Confederacy:
The Struggle for the Southern Backcountry

Teaching for Recall & Analysis:
New Strategies for Improving Student Achievement in Social
Studies

Teaching for Recall & Analysis:
Advanced Interactive Venn Diagrams for U.S. History

Teaching for Recall & Analysis:
Advanced Floor Timelines for U.S. History

Teaching for Recall & Analysis:
Improving Student Achievement in World History

www.ingramcontent.com/pod-product-compliance
Lightning Source LLC
Chambersburg PA
CBHW052035270326
41931CB00012B/2503